SONS

OF

GOD

Sons

of

Life-giving Communication
with the Spirit of God

God

Dixie Choyce

WinePressPublishing
Your Book, Defined. Since 1991.

© 2010 by Dixie Choyce. All rights reserved.

WinePress Publishing (PO Box 428, Enumclaw, WA 98022) functions only as book publisher. As such, the ultimate design, content, editorial accuracy, and views expressed or implied in this work are those of the author.

No part of this publication may be reproduced, stored in a retrieval system, or transmitted in any way by any means—electronic, mechanical, photocopy, recording, or otherwise—without the prior permission of the copyright holder, except as provided by USA copyright law.

Unless otherwise noted, all scriptures are taken from the *King James Version* of the Bible.

Scripture references marked NIV are taken from the *Holy Bible, New International Version, NIV,* Copyright 1973, 1978, 1984 by Biblica, Inc. Used by permission of Zondervan. All rights reserved wordwide. www.Zondervan.com

Scripture references marked NASB are taken from the *New American Standard Bible,* © 1960, 1963, 1968, 1971, 1972, 1973, 1975, 1977 by The Lockman Foundation. Used by permission.

ISBN 13: 978-1-4141-1746-1
ISBN 10: 1-4141-1746-9
Library of Congress Catalog Card Number: 2010902977

This manuscript is dedicated to all those who want to read it and share it with others. I hope that these samples of my experiences and thoughts in my walk with the Lord will enrich yours as much as the experiences and thoughts of others have often enriched mine.

You have my permission to copy, print, publish, or translate it into other languages as long as you do not omit any part of it, add to it or change anything in it. Please make your price for this book as low as you can to encourage more sales and readers. Together we will help others know Jesus better in their daily walk with Him.

Contents

Introduction ix

1. Did God Say Write a Book? 1
2. Hearing God 7
3. Educated Confusion 11
4. Investigating Facts 15
5. Obey God's Voice 21
6. Door to Tongues 25
7. Speaking in Tongues 29
8. The Northern Lights 35
9. Examples of Hearing God 39
10. God Talks to Everyone 43
11. Commitment to God's Plan 47
12. The Prayer of Commitment 55
13. Is It Really You, God? 61
14. Learning from the Past 67
15. Recent Events 75
16. Trusting God 79
17. Lord of the Storms 89
18. Distractions, Offenses, and Forgiveness 95
19. Strongholds to Be Broken 105

INTRODUCTION

THIS BOOK IS my attempt to convince ordinary Christians of the fact that they can have two-way communication with God. They are going to need this source of help to live through difficult coming trials. I am an ordinary Christian, but the experiences I have had in my ninety years on earth have shown me that even I can have spectacular experiences with God. I want to share my experiences with you so that you may be encouraged to seek the ability of hearing from God.

The church as a whole has not made Jesus' Great Commission our number one goal. Most of us have put our personal goals ahead of finding our part in carrying out the commission to get the gospel to every living person on earth. We seem to be entering now into a final battle between Satan and God. Many of us are looking for the rapture to take us out of that final struggle, but Jesus said that the last thing we must do before He comes is to get the gospel to all the world (see Matt. 24:14). The church is beginning now to move in that direction. We certainly have the equipment to get the job done. God has a special assignment for each one of us. Have you found yours?

CHAPTER 1

DID GOD SAY WRITE A BOOK?

ON THE MORNING of November 14, 2001, while I was in prayer, God answered my question regarding a prophecy given me by Cheryl Schang on the evening of November 11 at the end of her teaching in our church, Cornerstone Community Church in Mountlake Terrace, Washington. She had taught on Friday evening and all day Saturday and again on Sunday evening about how to move in the prophetic ministry, including the revelation gifts, and how to cast out demons. At the end of each session, we were allowed to practice what we had learned.

On Sunday morning, Cheryl came to ask about my ministry. I told her that I am ninety now, but in my youth I longed to have something big to do for the Lord. I would plead with Him to show me something really important to do for Him. I would be impressed to open the Bible. I'd find myself looking at Habakkuk 2:3, "For the vision is yet for an appointed time, but at the end it shall speak, and not lie: though it tarry, wait for it; because it will surely come, it will not tarry." These experiences of pleading with the Lord and then opening the Bible to Habakkuk 2:3 happened many times. At any other time, when I wanted to reflect more on the verse, I would never be able to find it. It was years later, when I undertook a major study of the Old Testament prophets, that I discovered the location of that verse.

Sons of God

I told her that around forty years ago, I was praying for a long list of people, and the Lord said that He wanted me to throw away that prayer list. I asked, "Why? I am getting results." He said, "I am going to teach you to pray for the things I want you to pray for. I want you to lift your sights from the details of people's lives. I am going to have you pray for nations, politicians, issues, missionaries, ministries, and big events in the world. Of course, you will pray for individuals at times, but I want to teach you to hear my voice directing your prayers. Intercession will be your main ministry."

The first thing He had me pray for was that China would open to the rest of the world so that we could get the gospel in. Eventually, under President Nixon, China opened. God also had me pray for Christian television to start. I heard about Pat Robertson's struggle to get started and I prayed for him. Then I heard about Paul and Jan Crouch's struggle to get TBN started and I prayed for them.

God lays many political things and ministries on my mind. I first pray in tongues, and then in English as He guides. After I had been doing this for a while, the Lord said, "This is the vision you were waiting for. I had to bring you to the point where you could do it." The ability to be directed by God in prayer was the answer to my youthful prayer for something big to do for God.

I told Cheryl that recently God had told me that He is going to make my house a house of prayer—that I am to spend more time in prayer and eventually He will send people for me to help in prayer. I am not to seek them. Right now He has sent me only one. She comes once a week and we pray together.

On Sunday night after we finished ministry to individuals, Cheryl gave personal prophecies to anyone who wanted this ministry. It was taped as given. She prayed for guidance before speaking. Her prophecy to me was as follows:

"Do you keep a journal?"

I said no.

She said, "You are supposed to keep a journal. You are supposed to begin to write."

I said that recently I had been recording and filing prophecies if they seem to be important.

Did God Say Write a Book?

She said, "It is not about prophecy to you. It is about truth, the treasures God has given you. There are some things inside you that most of us don't know. God has taught you some things that the rest of the world needs to know. Begin writing down what God has shown you: how to do things, how to figure things out, how to pray in certain areas, how to hear God in certain situations. You have all of those gifts and treasures inside of you, and the Lord wants them written down so they can be shared with many other people. It is an inheritance that you are going to leave to the generations. It is a very rich inheritance. You have paid a lot to get this, and it is worth a lot. It is life or death to some people. The Lord wants to pass it on to generations. So write down what the Lord has shown you.

"You are beginning now to mentor this woman. Write down the things you are putting into her and forming in her. Write down the things that should be taught to others, and it will be your inheritance to pass on."

I said that I took a course in adult writing for seven years, but nothing came of it, and Cheryl said, "Now you know why you did that."

For three days after Cheryl's prophecy, I prayed, asking God for confirmation any way He wanted to give it if it was really Him speaking to me. I told Him that writing is very hard work, and I did not want to write another book that never gets published. I did not want to waste time if His ministry for me is just intercessory prayer and working with the few people He sends to me.

For some time I had been thinking about the possibility of writing a book with the title, *That Voice*, with the theme of the common human error of rejecting the direct guidance of the Holy Spirit. This is what happened when the Israelites told Moses not to let God speak to them again, just get the rules from God and they would follow them (see Exodus 20:18-19). Most people do not seem to believe they can hear from God, and so they do not try. They prefer to have some religious leader give them rules to follow, or give them a personal word from God. I told God that if He really wanted me to write a book, I hoped He would write it. I needed guidance every step of the way.

After receiving the prophecy, I bought a notebook in which to keep a journal. I was prepared to write down what God said when He got around to giving me the answer to my question. On the third morning while I was praying, in tongues and in English, He finally started talking to me about it.

He said, "Do your writing on the computer instead of in that notebook, so that when it is time to write the book, you will have the material already so it will not have to be written twice. You can just make changes as needed. The title of the book will be *Sons Of God,* and not *That Voice.* I want the emphasis to be on the people who learn to hear my voice and follow my directions and not on the voice. The title will be based on Romans 8:14, 'For as many as are led by the Spirit of God, they are the sons of God.' He reminded me that after my mother died when I was a child, I used to climb the Evangeline Oak in Aunt Ida's yard and sing the songs my mother sang, especially one that said in part, "Hello Central, give me heaven, for my mamma's there. You will find her with the angels on the golden stairs. She'll be glad it's me who's speaking on the telephone."

I would wonder whether it might be possible that some day someone would invent a way for us to speak to heaven. Later when as an adult, I received the baptism of the Holy Spirit and was able to fluently interpret my tongue, I thought, "We really do have a way to speak to heaven and hear from God."

He reminded me also that in my meditations in that oak tree, I would wonder what life was for. I would picture the long line of generations. Babies are born, grow up, get married, do a lot of working, fighting, having fun, then they die, and another generation goes through this cycle. Why? What for? Then one day when I was twelve, two years after my mother's death, I was taking a bath and looking for something to read. I found the poem by Henry Wadsworth Longfellow (1807-1882), "A Psalm of Life." It seemed to answer all of my questions about a purpose for life. I memorized it.

The professor of one of my English classes in college referred to that poem as an example of "corn". In that era, "corn" was a slang word for something that was trite, insignificant, commonplace and boring. She called it "corn" because it had perfect rhythm and rhyme, but she missed the meaning of the poem. I did not memorize it according to rhythm and rhyme. I memorized it according to meaning. Thus:

Did God Say Write a Book?

Tell me not, in mournful numbers, life is but an empty dream! For the soul is dead that slumbers, and things are not what they seem.

Life is real! Life is earnest, and the grave is not its goal. Dust thou art to dust returneth was not spoken of the soul.

Not enjoyment, and not sorrow, is our destined end or way; but to act, that each to-morrow finds us farther than to-day.

Art is long, and time is fleeting, and our hearts, though stout and brave, still, like muffled drums, are beating funeral marches to the grave.

In the world's broad field of battle, in the bivouac of life, be not like dumb driven cattle. Be a hero in the strife.

Trust no Future, howe'er pleasant! Let the dead Past bury its dead! Act—act in the living present! Heart within, and God o'erhead!

Lives of great men all remind us we can make our lives sublime, and, departing, leave behind us footprints on the sands of time;

Footprints, that perhaps another, sailing o'er life's solemn main, a forlorn and shipwrecked brother, seeing shall take heart again.

Let us, then, be up and doing with a heart for any fate; still achieving, still pursuing, learn to labor and to wait.

Longfellow's poem became my goal, to live my life in such a way that I would add something to the progress of human relationships and Christianity. Later I became interested in writing and wanted to write something that would help future generations and thus I would leave my footprint on the sands of time. I knew that I was not able to write anything worthwhile until I had learned a lot more than I knew as a young person. After I wrote two books that I could not publish, and then two short ones that I did not even try to find a publisher for, I gave up. One publisher offered to publish the first book if I paid the cost. I found an editor who was eager to publish the second book, a biography. However, the man I wrote about would not allow the publication of his story, even though he had given me hours of his time and approved of it chapter by chapter. The third and fourth books were short fiction stories based on my experience with young people and children. I felt that all of this and other writings were just practice for writing the real book some day. Could this one be it?

After reminding me of this, God said to me that He put that desire to write in me, but He did not allow me to have anything published because I was not ready to write what He wanted written. He said that He had been training me all of these years, and now it was time to prepare to write His book.

Chapter 2

Hearing God

RECENTLY GOD TOLD me that He wanted me to pray in tongues and keep listening for His instructions all through the day, even when I am busy with other things. I said that I thought I was doing that, but He said it was not enough. That day while in the swimming pool exercising with the arthritis class, I tried to keep speaking in tongues without moving my mouth and still communicate with others when appropriate. I remembered that Jackie Pullinger said in her book, *Chasing The Dragon,* that she could not do all the miraculous things she did in her ministry with drug addicts in Hong Kong if she did not pray in tongues all of the time. If she can do it, I should be able to.

However, she said this to a young man who wanted to learn from her how to minister to the drug addicts. She took him with her on one of her daily trips of street ministry. He was embarrassed because she was chattering in tongues as they walked along or rode on public transportation. She would turn aside to minister to someone as the Holy Spirit guided her. No doubt she meant that by speaking in tongues as she progressed along her way, the Holy Spirit was able to get her attention and guide her to a person who would respond to her attempt to help.

Of course, we know that we cannot speak in tongues all of the time because we have to give attention to the job at hand or the conversation of the moment. However, if we daily commit every moment to God's plan and purpose and speak in tongues and in English as He guides, we are truly praying without ceasing and experiencing the joy and peace that accompany living in God's kingdom.

Jackie Pullinger decided when she was a young child that she wanted to be a missionary. However, when she grew up and tried to volunteer for missions, the mission boards refused to send her anywhere because she was under twenty-five years of age and unmarried. She took ship passage to the orient, expecting God to guide her to His destination. She persuaded the captain to let her off at Hong Kong with only one hundred dollars in her possession.

She taught music for income while working as a self-appointed missionary until people started handing her money from mysterious sources. The missionaries there told her that she could not win anyone to Christ because China had a spiritual cloud over it. She, however, succeeded where they failed. She would go into the Walled City where the police did not dare to go because the criminals and drug addicts were in control there. She had no fear of going there in the middle of the night and was safe even in dens where men were smoking opium. She became known as someone who wanted to help them, so they protected her. She would take converts into her home to teach them how to live like human beings and Christians, and was so successful that the government gave her a building to use for the rehabilitation of these former criminals.

I am aware that people who do not pray in tongues can hear from God. We have well-known spiritual leaders who do not choose to speak in tongues, or keep it secret if they do. I know that I heard from God before I spoke in tongues, but I hear from Him far more often now that I do.

We are so proud of our free will and our ability to reason things out for ourselves that these things get in the way of hearing God's voice. The very act of speaking in an unknown tongue allows the Holy Spirit to bypass the intellect. We speak in tongues because we really want to submit our wills to God's will. The Holy Spirit then prays or speaks to us according to the Father's will. We interpret the tongue under the guidance of the Holy Spirit and find that God's prayer or word to us was better than our intellects could have produced (see Rom. 8:14).

Hearing God

When I was eighteen, Mrs. Buckley (my Southern Baptist minister's wife, at Istrouma Baptist Church in Baton Rouge, Louisiana) was my Sunday school teacher. Her natural features were very unattractive, but when she stood to teach us about our Lord, her face shone with such radiance that she became beautiful. I always wondered what that light was that seemed to come from under her skin.

She became my personal mentor when I was pressured to teach her class of girls my own age because she became too ill to continue. She taught me to pray about it and lean on the Holy Spirit to do the teaching. I knew I could not do it without His help. I would say, "God, I can't do this. You will have to do it." I studied and prayed all week and ran to her for teaching. Then, when I stood before that class looking to Him for guidance, He took over, and I felt that powerful presence of the Holy Spirit speaking through me, sometimes surprising myself by what I said.

After Mrs. Buckley was well enough to be up, she asked me to be her prayer partner, and we would meet in the old wooden church building and pray for the many problems and people needing prayer. We rejoiced over many answered prayers.

We prayed fervently for a new building even though it seemed absolutely impossible in the worst part of the depression of the 1930s. God amazed us by having the top managers of the local Standard Oil Company send our pastor to New York to see John D. Rockefeller himself. Rockefeller promised to give us $10,000 if we could raise another $10,000. Another surprise. We did it! Then he matched another $10,000, and laborers donated one day of labor out of six. We got a brick building without a mortgage.

After the building was completed, I was asked to be the superintendent of the Young People's Department of the Sunday school—a department that did not yet exist. I had to first organize it. I did this until the pastor went back to school in Texas. Shortly after that, I moved near my work as a telephone operator and started classes at the Louisiana State University.

Chapter 3

Educated Confusion

NOW I WANT to recall some of the later things that happened leading up to my learning to improve my ability to listen for God's guidance in prayer, and some of my experiences in prayer after I started trying to pray God's way.

My six years of college education and two college degrees under liberal thinking professors brought a lot of doubts into my understanding of spiritual things. I learned to carry my education in one pocket of my mind and my faith in another, and it did not work very well. At first, I was very busy working full time and going to school full time, then part time work and full time school. This left almost no time for Bible study and prayer. I would think, "I'll get back to that." When rarely I did, God flooded me with his presence, and I would wonder why I did not do it more often because it was so glorious, as if He were saying, "Where have you been? I've been here all the time."

I made some terrible decisions during those years, and also during the following years when I did social work. I got back into church and Bible reading and prayer at the end of World War II when I met Stan and moved to Seattle where Stan lived. He had sent me information on children's agencies, and I got a job as a children's caseworker at Washington Children's Home. We were married and later adopted a baby girl, Colleen, and then a baby boy, Stephen.

Sons of God

My husband and I attended a spiritually dead Congregational Church because they had a Sunday school program that was attractive to us for our daughter. The program was advertised through an article in the newspaper. I discovered shortly that anyone I talked to in that church about prayer reacted similarly. It was obvious that they thought prayer was good thoughts or good deeds. I became desperate and one day asked, "Lord, isn't there anyone left in the world that believes the Bible as I do?" He said, "Be patient, and in about two years you will meet a woman who will lead you to a group that believes the way you do."

In the meantime, I decided to resolve the conflict between my education and my faith once and for all. I do not recommend that anyone else do what I did because it opened the door for Satan to do some devilment in our family. However, I prayed for guidance and protection all the way through and wound up with an unshakable faith in God and the absolute truth of every word of the Bible. I decided to investigate all the things other than Christianity in which people put their faith.

There really is ". . . none other name [than Jesus'] under heaven given among men, whereby we must be saved" (Acts 4:12). Other religions offer a better way to relate to other people and demon gods to fear, but they cannot bring peace and joy in a personal relationship with the Creator God who died for our sins, and rose again to prove it.

I also discovered that there is something to all those things like spiritualism, numerology, fortune-telling, and divination of all kinds. God's creation is based on mathematical formulas, and it is possible to use our God-given intellects to discover them and to apply them in the spiritual realm. However, God forbids this kind of experimentation because it opens the door for demons to possess or harass us and to deceive us. When you try to contact a deceased person, you get a demon. When you depend on any of these things, you are disobeying God, who should be the One to guide you in everything. If you want to be miserable, try them, but if you want to have a wonderful life in the security of God's presence, give it all to God, no matter how treacherous life seems to be at the moment.

Educated Confusion

While praying once for people trapped in the New Age Movement, which draws largely on Hinduism and Buddhism, God said to me, "If America wants India's gods, America can have India's poverty. If India wants America's Christian God, India can have America's prosperity."

Chapter 4

Investigating Facts

SINCE IT WAS so-called scientific facts that had caused my confusion in the first place, I decided it was time to see how many of the teachings on evolution were based on real facts. My first college degree was from a teachers' college. I majored in English and history, and my graduate degree was a Master of Social Work. I had taken only the required science courses in high school and college, so I needed to broaden my knowledge in that area. I started with biology, since evolution was based on our supposed descent from monkeys or apes and prior to that from lower forms of life.

I went to the library and took out a biology textbook and read it, and then others. The central part of my search was to find any known provable fact that refuted anything in the Bible. I discovered that every reference to evolution was based on a hypotheses or an unproved theory or supposition. I found it was a known fact that every movement in life from cell to the outside of the body was started from the outside. So what was the movement from the outside that caused the body to move? God? About the time I read this, I saw an article in the newspaper that stated scientists had discovered there is a light coming into the universe from some unknown source. Again, is this God's light? Another known fact is that the whole universe is expanding at a known rate of speed and another fact is that everything is breaking down from larger to smaller units, not building up as required for evolution to be a fact. These known facts confirmed Bible statements.

Every textbook I read stated that we know the age of the fossils of the past because we know the age in which each layer of sediment laid down in the earth in which the fossils are found. Lower forms of life are at the bottom, and higher ones appear in ascending order. How do we know the age of those layers? The science of geology gives us those ages, so the biologists said.

Since geology was so important to the proof of evolution, it was time to study geology. I could not believe what I read in the first book, so I read two more geology textbooks by different authors. All three made the same statements, "Geology is a new science. It is only about one hundred years old. We do not know anything. We are guessing. How do we know the age of the layers of deposits in the earth? We know the age of each layer because of the type of fossils in it." In addition, it seems that the layers are not always in the same order. They may be upside down in some areas, or there may be only some of them present in others. By this system of circular reasoning, we arrive at the age of our supposed ancestors and the age of the earth. Biologists prove the age of the fossils by reference to the age the geologists assign to the layers of deposits in which the fossils are found and the geologists determined the age of a given layer of deposit by age of the type of fossils found in it! And we are supposed to believe this bunch of guessers?

I next studied physics, then astronomy and some general science books, but nowhere did I find anything that refuted anything in the Bible with an absolutely known fact. Toward the end of all of this research I discovered that there are several organizations of scientists with multiple college degrees who believe that the known scientific facts refute evolution and support creation and God as the creator. They have continuing research projects that uncover more and more evidence that the Bible is accurate in all of its scientific statements made prior to their discovery by modern scientists. The book of Job has many of these.

I regularly receive news from the Institute of Creation Research (ICR) and their college for graduate students. They publish many books for young and old. They reported that the evolutionists refused to debate with Dr. Gish, because they always lost the debate. Dr. Duane

Investigating Facts

Gish (Ph.D. in biochemistry from University of California at Berkley) is currently retired from ICR, but continues some speaking and writing. ICR has honored him by giving him the title of Senior Vice President Emeritus.

Dr. Carl Baugh, who has Creation Evidences Museum in Glen Rose, Texas, has a program on Trinity Broadcasting Network. His museum contains fossils with evidence of a recent creation. He also has a machine that simulates conditions as they would have been at the beginning of life on earth. He presents scientific evidence that the conditions of earth in the beginning were much better than now, with healthier, longer life spans for people, animals, and plants. Those conditions have gradually diminished. He and the scientists at the Institute of Creation Research believe that the earth is between six and ten thousand years old.

On a recent program, Dr. Baugh mentioned a study of the magnetic field around the earth, which is known to be losing strength. Every fourteen hundred years it is reduced to half its strength. Recently, because of this reduction in strength, birds may not always be able to find their way in migration. In another eight hundred years, life will be unbearable. If you go back to twice the strength of the magnetic field every fourteen hundred years, you reach a point in six to ten thousand years where life could not exist, because the orientation of all living things depends on the level of strength of the magnetic field. Another mathematical calculation by an expert in algebra shows that if you trace the rate of expansion of the universe backward, you arrive at zero in about six to ten thousand years.

Dr. Baugh said that in a recent conversation with an evolutionist, he presented these two studies and asked for the evolutionist's reaction. He said, "Well, we know that evolution is a fact. Therefore, the universe has to be billions of years old for evolution to have happened." All of the leading evolutionists seem to have this Archie Bunker kind of reasoning, "Don't confuse me with the facts. My head is made up." They have control of the educational system in our country and force the teaching of evolution as an irrefutable fact, offering no opportunity for the presentation of facts that disprove it. Years ago I read somewhere that one of the famous Huxleys said, "We have to believe in evolution. If we had to believe that there is a Creator God, we would have to repent of our sexual sins." More Archie Bunker reasoning: "As long as we say we do not believe in God, we are not accountable for our sins."

The evolutionists know that if it were true that one species develops into a higher form, there would have to be fossils of intermediate life forms, or "missing links." Actually, there should be many thousands of them. Over the last couple of centuries a few evolutionists have claimed to have discovered a "missing link," and there is great celebration over proving that man really did descend from apes. However, their "missing link" is always proven to be a deliberate hoax.

The Bible seems to leave some opening for the possibility that there have been other cycles of creation. In the first chapter of Genesis, did God create the heaven and the earth and then did it suffer some kind of destruction between verses one and two? When He told Adam and Eve to replenish the earth, does it mean that the earth had previously been filled with people or other kinds of life?

Does the Bible indicate that we are coming to the end of one cycle of life on earth and there may be others? Hebrews 1:10-12 says, "And Thou, Lord, in the beginning hast laid the foundation of the earth; and the heavens are the works of thine hands: They shall perish; but thou remainest; and they all shall wax old as doth a garment; and as a vesture shalt thou fold them up, and they shall be changed: but thou art the same, and thy years shall not fail." Second Peter 3:10-13 tells us that when Jesus comes, the earth and the heavens will be burned up. Revelation 21:1-3 tells us that at this point there will be a new heaven and a new earth, with the New Jerusalem coming down to earth. God will dwell with us. But what will we be doing? Will we be supervising a new population of life on the new earth? We need to prepare now for whatever our responsibilities will be then. We cannot know all the answers to those questions now, but we will when we see Him face to face. "For now we see through a glass, darkly; but then face to face: now I know in part; but then shall I know even as also I am known" (1 Cor. 13:12).

We have many proofs that the Bible is literally the Word of God dictated by the Holy Spirit to authors He chose, and all of His authors were Jews except for the gentile physician, Luke, who wrote the book of Luke and the book of Acts. Luke was a close companion of the early

Investigating Facts

Jewish believers. Satan hates the Jews and Christian believers because they are God's chosen instruments to tell the world about Him. Satan sponsors false religions and inspires the followers of these religions to persecute Jews and Christians.

Through the years of my searching for proof that my faith is based on real truth, I have read of the many ways in which God has verified the fact that He wrote the Bible. I am convinced that the one who created everything is able to write his workbook exactly the way He wanted it written.

Grant R. Jeffrey has summed up all of these proofs in his book, *The Signature of God*, better than any other source I have read. He reviews all of the archaeological discoveries that prove the accuracy of historical and other statements in the Bible. He reviews the hundreds of prophecies in the Bible that have been fulfilled, including those about Jesus' heritage, birth, life, ministry, death, and resurrection, and those sure to be fulfilled. He reviews the work of Ivan Panin, a former atheist from the USSR. I had read about Panin's work some twenty years ago. He discovered a mathematical pattern throughout the original text of both Old and New Testaments that cannot be duplicated in any other work, and cannot be imitated by doubters.

I learned from Jeffrey's book about the hidden numerical codes in the original Hebrew text of the Bible. This was discovered originally in the fourteenth century by Rabbeynu Bachayah, but not pursued. During the World War II years, Rabbi Michael Dov Weissmand pursued this finding and discovered many hidden codes in the Torah. The invention of the computer made it easier to find the codes. Dedicated scholars in mathematics and computer science at the Hebrew University and the Jerusalem College of Technology have expanded the study.

Even mathematical scientists who do not believe in God admit that these findings are valid and cannot be duplicated from any other texts. Secular scientists and mathematicians in other colleges and universities have admitted that no human being could have produced this phenomenon.

Hebrew researchers have discovered the codes throughout all of the text of the original Scriptures that Christians call the Old Testament. The codes found in the earliest written books of the Old Testament sometimes referred to events that would happen in later Jewish history and to people who lived centuries later. When the events happened, they were recorded in books of the Old Testament or New Testament written centuries later. There are references to recent wars and modern people by name and events associated with them. These references can only be found after the event. They do not foretell the future until after it occurs.

The code works by finding the first letter of a word and moving on in the text until you find the second letter, then the rest. If these letters are equally spaced, every third letter, or fourth or whatever, you know you have a hidden message. So you continue searching for the rest of the message in the same spacing of letters. Some codes are found by searching the text backward.

Some codes refer to events during the time between Old and New Testament. Hebrew Scripture has the name of Jesus in many places. All of his apostles are named and other numerous people and events in the New Testament. In the fifty-third chapter of Isaiah referring to Jesus' death on the cross, there is a code stating, "My name is Jeshuah (Jesus)."

There are many coded references to modern events and people. For instance in the book of Deuteronomy, there are many references to the Nazi Holocaust, Hitler, Eichmann, Berlin, names of the death camps, Auschwitz and Belsen, etc. There are coded references to Desert Storm in Genesis, with names, Saddam, George Bush, Schwarzkopf, America being "in Iraq," "in Saudi Arabia" and other names connected with that war. Anwar Sadat's assassination is in code with the date 1981 and the words president, gunfire, shot, murder, and the name of the person responsible. In Genesis there are also coded names and references to Arafat and Rabin and in Deuteronomy, Rabin's assassination. Anyone with an open mind should know that we are nearing the end and that Jesus is coming soon to set up his kingdom.

Chapter 5

Obey God's Voice

YOU HEAR A lot of people quoting Romans 8:28, "All things work together for good to them that love God, to them who are the called according to his purpose." People have told me that God turned all the bad things that happened to me for good. Sure, I agree that He did when I finally started trying to live all of my life for Him. However, the mistake here is in not knowing that the word "things" was a misleading translation of the Greek word, which means "a divine expression" or a "word from God." The whole passage is telling you how to be guided by the Holy Spirit in order to follow God's purpose for your decisions.

The verse is really the conclusion of the thoughts in the two verses preceding it. "Likewise the Spirit also helpeth our infirmities: for we know not what we should pray for as we ought: but the Spirit itself maketh intercession for us with groanings which cannot be uttered. And he that searcheth the hearts knoweth what is the mind of the Spirit, because he maketh intercession for the saints according to the will of God" (Rom. 8:26-27). Now verse 28: "And we know that all things work together for good to them that love God, to them who are the called according to his purpose." The "things," in this verse, could be a word or message from God. It could be God highlighting a verse of Scripture, making us hear a word mentally, or giving us a feeling to do or not do something.

Sons of God

I will give you an instance where a young woman got into trouble because she did not obey that still small voice warning her not to take a shortcut to her apartment after a run for exercise. She thought she was so close to God that she would know how to handle anyone who attempted to harm her. She ignored the feeling that she should not take the shortcut and was grabbed by a man who raped her. All through the experience she was calling on God and pleading the blood of Jesus while talking to the man to dissuade him, but nothing worked. Did that experience work for her good? No! It was the nudge not to take the route she chose that would have worked for her good. However, God made good come out of it because she was calling on Him throughout the experience, she did not suffer the trauma that others have suffered from like experiences.

If I had always been seeking God's guidance and following His Bible and His whispered word to me, I could have saved myself a lot of misery and could have followed His preferred plan for my life. Now that I keep myself in close touch with God, every day is filled with peace and joy (usually) no matter what is happening around me. Of course, I am not perfect at trusting God in the midst of a trial—even a small one, but I know that this is the goal toward which I am working.

Philippians 4:6-7 tells us to, "Be careful (or anxious) for nothing; but in every thing by prayer and supplication with thanksgiving let your requests be made known unto God. And the peace of God, which passeth all understanding, shall keep your hearts and minds through Christ Jesus."

When I become frustrated or anxious about something I have misplaced, or over errors on the computer with which I need help, I know it is time to draw aside and commit the problem to God. "Lord, you know where those car keys are and whether you want me to find them. If you do not want me to find them, it's O.K. I'll get another set made. Just lead me to them your way, or tell me if you want me to have another set made. Praise your name. I want you in charge of every detail of my life." Then my peace returns, and shortly the problem is solved. In the case of the car keys, I seemed impressed to examine again the things I take to the pool, and I found the keys in the toe of the sandals I wear between locker and pool.

Obey God's Voice

I ask the Lord to help me with shopping needs and to save me a convenient parking space. I ask far enough ahead of time so that He can have me arrive just in time to get one in front of the building I need to enter. He is always faithful. He really is interested in everything we do if we are interested in pleasing Him as well.

In bigger problems, I am not ready to deal with the situation until I know I am in the center of the peace that comes from trusting God and receiving His guidance. The night that Stan had his massive stroke, I knew at once what had happened and I sent up a quick prayer for help. Then I called our hospital and 911 and turned it over to them. I was too numb to be in charge, but God heard my cry for help and sent a Christian neighbor I hardly knew. She took charge of me and got me into the ambulance with my necessary personal things—my Bible, my church directory, her phone number, and assurance of prayers.

Chapter 6

Door to Tongues

TWO YEARS AFTER God had told me that in two years I would meet a woman who would lead me to a group which believed the way I did, our neighbor Jim disappeared suddenly, leaving his wife with three preschool-aged children and no income. Many neighbors tried to help, and in the midst of this problem, I saw an article in the newspaper about Agnes Sanford, who would be holding a week of meetings on prayer and miracles in an Episcopal church. I knew without a doubt that this was the woman God told me about.

I called a neighbor who attended a neighborhood Episcopal church and suggested that we go to those meetings and pray for Jim. Five of us went all week and discovered later that we had all prayed the same thing, not that Jim would come home, but that he would come to his senses and get the help he needed. Months later, Jim returned and explained that he had amnesia during his absence and came to himself enough to know he needed help. He was admitted to a mental hospital until he recovered his memory. He dated the time of realizing he needed help. It was the week of our prayer sessions with Agnes Sanford.

Agnes Sanford announced that she would be holding a teaching retreat on healing prayer for five days at a Christian resort that summer, 1960. I went to the retreat and learned many things that helped me go deeper with God in my prayer life—more than I could ever recall now, but was able to put into practice.

One thing that stood out in my memory was the warning that in order to keep the channel open to God for answered prayer, we must be very careful never to let the slightest hint of sin or disobedience cloud the channel to God. She gave an illustration in her own life of putting a slight dent in a telephone company truck and calling the company to report it. It cost her three dollars to get it fixed. She could have said to herself, "Oh well, they have insurance to cover that," and she could have forgotten about it. But the incident buried in her subconscious would have been a block to her relationship with God. Actually, the driver called and thanked her and explained that he would have had to pay for the repair.

Remembering that warning, if a clerk gives me a little too much change or a store rings up a loss to them, I set the matter straight. I want to be totally honest in all things because I do not want any block between God and me.

Agnes Sanford taught that when we pray for a healing, we should get a picture in our minds of the healing taking place. She said that cancer is a different kind of healing. Cells are multiplying, and we must picture the Holy Spirit coming on the area as a fire burning out the multiplying cells. The same picture must be used to burn out germ cells. Pray for this to happen.

Stan and I had occasion to use this kind of prayer for a woman in our home group in the latter part of the 1970s. I was scheduled to spend the day with her at the hospital, and the day before my turn, Stan insisted that we go together to see her. She was alone and very frightened because the doctors told her that morning that they had cleaned out the infection during her heart surgery as best they could, and if healing had not started by the time they returned in the afternoon, there would be nothing more they could do. I told her to picture the Holy Spirit burning the infection out. We prayed for this to happen. Later in the day, the doctor found that the wound was cleansing itself.

During the teaching retreat on prayer, I had a personal interview with Agnes Sanford to talk about many traumatic experiences in my childhood. She was a great help. At the end of our time, she laid her

Door to Tongues

hands on my head and prayed, and for the first time in my life, I felt the warmth of the Holy Spirit coursing throughout my body like a gentle electrical current. I felt like a new person afterward.

At the end of our meetings, we had a final meeting with communion, and all of our teachers prayed individually for us. Agnes Sanford prayed for me to receive the gift of joy.

After I got home, I found myself often singing joyful praise songs and sometimes was surprised to find that a foreign syllable would slip into the song. My children asked why, and I would say, "Oh, just for fun." It actually was joyful when it happened. Later I realized that this was the beginning of my receiving the gift of tongues.

Chapter 7

Speaking in Tongues

I MET THREE women at Agnes Sanford's retreat who attended our neighborhood Episcopal Church. I accepted their invitation to join their weekly prayer group, which had been formed at the request of Father J., the pastor. He told Peggy, the leader, that he did not have time to pray for all of the people who requested his prayers. He had Peggy's group come to communion on Wednesday mornings and then have their own Bible study prayer meeting and pray for his long list of needs.

We made our own lists of the prayer requests to take home, as well as praying as a group. We agreed to spend every morning from 9:00 to 9:15 praying for those prayer requests. We had many positive answers to our prayers, including miracles of healing for cancer, even when the doctors had given up.

I learned later that Agnes Sanford and the two Episcopal priests who helped her teach the classes all had the gift of tongues, but she was afraid that if she told anyone she spoke in tongues, she would be kicked out of the church. They felt us out individually, and if we seemed open to receive, they would privately help anyone who wanted to receive the gift. Peggy felt the power, but held back from speaking in tongues because she feared her husband's reaction.

Father W. mentioned to me what had happened to Father Dennis Bennett, an Episcopal priest and rector of a large Episcopal Church in

California, when he started speaking in tongues. Miraculous things happened, but some of his staff and members of the church raised objections. He decided to resign rather than split the church. He was now the pastor of St. Luke's, a small Episcopal Church in the Ballard area of Seattle that had lost so many members it was now a mission kept going by contributions from the diocese.

Regarding tongues I asked, "What's it for?" Father W. apparently thought I was not open and did not invite me to learn more. I really just wanted to know why anyone needed to speak in tongues.

During the week of our retreat, all of the priests and the bishop of the Diocese of Seattle had been at a conference where Father Bennett, in late night informal meetings of any interested priests, shared his experiences of speaking in tongues. On his way home to Chicago, Father W., our teacher, stopped in Seattle to visit Father Bennett and his small group of interested members. He helped them all receive the baptism in the Holy Spirit. Father Bennett's book, *Nine O'Clock in the Morning* tells the whole story of his experiences and the sudden growth of St. Luke's, the little mission church, after it became alive with the powerful presence of the Holy Spirit. People from churches of all denominations from all over the Seattle area, and even from other states and countries, visited to see the miraculous things happening there and to share in God's glorious presence. Under Father Bennett's guidance, his little prayer group had not talked about their experience until their spiritual growth became so obvious that people around them demanded an explanation of the obvious change in them and wanted to join them.

Within a few months of my joining Peggy's prayer group, we began to hear of the things happening at St. Luke's—people being healed and lives changed. One by one we went to investigate. We learned that Father J. had been at the diocese conference and knew about the private discussions of the priests, but he was not interested in hearing about Dennis Bennett's experiences.

Within a short time almost all of Peggy's prayer group and our husbands received the baptism in the Holy Spirit and we started our own weekly evening prayer meetings. This group is mentioned as "The Northern Lights" in Dennis Bennett's book, *Nine O'Clock in the Morning*.

Speaking in Tongues

When we first started watching the miraculous things happening at St. Luke's and hearing about speaking in tongues, I was a little fearful of receiving. What if I said something I would not have said in English and someone else knew what I said, but I did not? Then in a morning class, Dennis allowed us to hear what it was like. Someone spoke quietly in a strange language and a woman leaning back against a basement supporting pillar quietly gave the interpretation. It sounded like a beautiful psalm of praise. I thought if that was what it was like, I wanted it. It was not at all like the big tent meetings I had seen as a child with people falling in the sawdust aisles and screaming. That was so undignified!

On the next Friday night, I went to their public prayer meeting to receive the Holy Spirit "with dignity." I sat in the midst of a group of enthusiastic students from a Christian college in Tacoma and I suggested they pray for me to receive. I am sure they did. That night was the only night I was ever given a long list of songs that had been planned for the service. Way down on the list I found, "Nearer My God To Thee," which I had never been able to sing without crying because it was sung at my six-month-old baby sister's funeral when I was five.

That baby, Elodie, was as precious to me as she would have been if she had been my baby, and the events of her death and funeral were forever stamped on my memory. My mother's milk gave out, and the doctor was unable to find a formula that Elodie could digest. Mama took her to New Orleans and went from doctor to doctor with no results. They told her that Elodie would die, so she brought her home together with a nurse.

In the early morning hours two weeks later, Mama and the nurse were with her. Mama said, "Elodie," and our baby turned and smiled and died with the smile on her face. They woke us up because they were clearing our large bedroom for the funeral service later that day, and I was put in a bed between my two sisters, Doris and Irma. Their bodies were too warm for me, and I lay there awake, wondering how they could sleep when Elodie was dead. My sorrow was greater than I thought I could bear.

When the little blue coffin was delivered, my mother cried more than she had earlier because the pillow was very hard. A neighbor grabbed the pillow and sped away to make a soft one. The smiling baby was still laid out in her crib wearing a long white dress with a white ribbon bow with long streamers. My cousin, Rosemond, and Aunt Ida arrived, and we children gathered around the crib and talked about Elodie. Each of them kissed her and told me to. I kissed her forehead and was shocked at the cold.

After a brief service, including the song, "Nearer My God to Thee," everyone went to the cemetery and stood around the grave under umbrellas in the pouring Louisiana rain. We watched the men lower the blue coffin into a pool of water and then shovel mud on it up to a heap of mud at the top.

I was in a deep depression for six months after Elodie's death until God gave me a dream of her. She was wearing the long white dress in which she was buried, but she had grown to be a two or three year old and was wearing hard-soled shoes. She was running around on our back porch so close to the edge that I feared she would fall off. I grabbed the long ribbons on the dress and screamed for help while she laughed at my fears, while leaning backward off the porch at a forty-five degree angle. I woke up and knew God had shown me that she was in a good place where she was growing, was happy, and did not want me to worry about her. I got over the depression, but I still could not sing that song without reliving the fear of losing family members in death, and I could not sing that song without crying.

I realized that God had put that song on that list for me to deal with, and I thought, *Oh no, why would He do that to me?* I made up my mind that I would sing it without tears, and I did, but I could not hit a single note right. I felt as if there was an electric current running through all of my blood vessels. My new friends led me upstairs to the altar, where two of the experienced older women helped me to begin speaking in tongues.

My blood was still on fire with the Holy Spirit, and I felt the presence of God as I was baptized in Him inside and out. I looked around to find Him because He had to be there somewhere. I asked my helpers what I was saying in that new language, and they said, "We can't interpret for other people. You speak again and then say, 'Thus saith the Lord,' and say whatever comes to mind in English. That is your interpretation."

Speaking in Tongues

(I learned later that it is not necessary to say, "Thus saith the Lord" to receive the interpretation. It will come if we just say the first words that come in English and more will follow until the message is complete. Sometimes I ask what it means.)

I followed instructions and heard myself saying, "I did not put you here to grieve. I put you here to serve. I have called you to a life of joy. Now live in joy. If you will keep praising My name and seeking Me in prayer, I will show you how to live a life of joy and peace." There was more that I cannot remember.

All the way home I spoke in tongues, and interpreted, and was bathed in the joyful presence of the Lord. I spent the next morning doing housework and speaking in tongues. I did not interpret, but I knew what I was doing. I was telling God off in my new language, as I would never have dared do in English. Why did He give me so much grief with family problems, personal problems, and the deaths of so many I dearly loved. In turn, He was giving me the correction I needed. I wound up on my knees, washing my hands of the whole thing, and thinking that this secretly rebellious woman had gone to be with God. I had always outwardly worked hard at being "good" like Mama said, but inside I was deeply hurt by the many offenses of others.

I continued to interpret my prayer language so fluently that I began to wonder whether I could be making it up. I went back to a Friday night prayer meeting at St. Luke's and asked one of the members to confirm this for me. We knelt at the altar and I spoke in tongues and interpreted and asked whether she heard what I did. She said she could not interpret for others but said, "I will get Betty. She hears English instead of the foreign language when you speak in tongues."

Betty knelt beside me, and I prayed, "Please, Lord, let me say exactly what I said before." Betty's interpretation was word for word what I had previously said. It was God telling me that I was not doing this, it was He, my God, who had been with me all of my life and had a plan for me that He wanted me to follow. There was much more that I cannot recall.

Another time when I was doubting my fluent interpretations, I found myself speaking words that were in poetic rhythm and stanzas. I interpreted, and sure enough it was a long poem of praise. I asked whether He was going to teach me to write poetry. He said He was not, but wanted to convince me that I was accurately interpreting everything He said.

On another morning of joyful praise I asked, "Lord, how do I really know that all of this is real? I am believing what I have been taught, but what proof do I have that it is really true?"

I was suddenly overwhelmed with His presence, and in my mind I could see Jesus standing beside me. I felt that if I opened my eyes, I would see Him. He said forcefully, "This is how you know! You have felt My presence many times, and you know by My presence and My messages to you that I am real. You will not feel My presence this powerfully very often, so any time you are inclined to doubt, *you remember this experience.*"

Chapter 8

The Northern Lights

MY HUSBAND AND I joined that spiritually dead Episcopal Church in our neighborhood because we wanted to be with our friends, The Northern Lights. We all had great hopes of getting the people in the church to discover the wonder of having two-way communication with God. Only a few responded favorably. Some complained to the pastor about us, but he told them, "I am not going to fight this because it is of God. I do not want any of it, and if you do not want it, stay away from it."

They called us Gladys' Glad Gang, and the pastor did not want to lose any of us because we were workers and givers. Gladys was the choir director and was a part of the Northern Lights. She had persuaded us to join the choir.

Once I was praying for different members of the church, urging God to help them receive the Holy Spirit so the whole church would be lit up with His presence, and God told me to stop. I asked why, and He said, "Let me show you something." I had a vivid mental vision of a very big, tall candle with a small light at the top. I had my head tilted far back looking at that light.

He said, "Do you see what you are doing? You are looking at the light at the top. The pastor is the one who will either light up the church or keep it in darkness. If you cannot pray the pastor in, this church will remain dead."

SONS OF GOD

Since our eagerness to win converts to the baptism in the Holy Spirit was raising more alarm than converts, the Northern Lights sought advice from some of the original prayer group at St. Luke's. Betty met with us and assured us that she knew how we felt because they were as eager as we were to share this joyful experience, but they had been guided to keep quiet about it until the rest of the church noticed a change in them and demanded an explanation. She said that people would look at their happy faces with curiosity but say nothing, at first. Eventually, one or two at a time inquired and were brought into their prayer meeting and received the gift of tongues. Thus their experience gradually became known to the whole church, and within months was known to people from many other churches, who came to see what was happening.

As we prayed together that evening, the Holy Spirit kept advising us to follow the example of being silent until questioned, but we kept saying things like, "But, what if…?" Again the Holy Spirit would advise us. Finally, I began speaking in tongues and laughing at the same time. It was obvious that God was laughing at us while He was speaking.

Betty, who hears English when someone speaks in tongues, interpreted, "Life is like a child learning to walk. His diapers are so bulky between his legs that he keeps falling down and has to get up and try again. Why can't you just go with the advice already given?"

Peggy had been holding back about receiving the baptism because her husband, Chuck, was opposed. He had even gone to the bishop to complain about St. Luke's. He was assured that this was an authentic move of God, but Chuck could make a choice about receiving it. Chuck continued to forbid Peggy to receive. I was in prayer one day and received this interpretation, "Tell Peggy to go ahead and receive. Chuck is mine. I will take care of him."

I debated for a few minutes about whether this really was God speaking, and whether I should call her or wait for her to speak to me about it. I was reaching for the telephone when she called and immediately said, "I want so badly to receive this gift, but I have to hold back until Chuck receives because he will be furious if I go before he does."

I told her the word I had just received. She was overjoyed and said she would go that night to the Friday night prayer meeting at St. Luke's and receive. Chuck told her again that she could not go to that meeting and hid the car keys. She fixed dinner for the family, picked up a can of diet food for herself, and searched through a bunch of keys until she found one that looked like a car key. She found it fit the first car she tried it on. Chuck sat down at the table with the children and he asked where their mother was. One of them pointed to the receding car. Chuck asked, "Oh, God, can you make car keys, too?"

Peggy received the gift of tongues at the altar and then went with a small group to a private home to continue in prayer. People were so excited about having two-way communication with God that they would have remained at the church all night. One man said, "We have a pipeline to heaven." When the church put them out at midnight, they would go in groups to private homes and pray until three or four in the morning.

When Peggy sneaked into bed with Chuck in the wee hours of the morning, he said, "Well, did you receive?" When she said she had, he demanded, "Let me hear you!"

On hearing her, he recognized that it was real. He still spent several weeks protesting the presence of this new experience in his church and his home. He finally decided that he would be willing to receive, but could not, no matter how hard he tried. Finally, he was driving down the highway one day and said, "Oh, God, I'm just a jerk." He hit the visor over his head and his Bible fell off it onto his head, and he started speaking in tongues.

Chapter 9

Examples of Hearing God

ONE THURSDAY MORNING during the communion service at St. Luke's, I was watching the priest and several people praying for a member of their prayer group who was kneeling at the altar. I asked, "Lord, is there anything I can do?" He told me to kneel behind the woman and put my hands on her legs and pray for her healing, but not to let her see me. He said she was unable to receive healing through her friends, but would receive if she did not know through whom she received. I did as instructed and got away quickly. Later, as a group of us talked outside the church, this woman described her experience of not being able to feel anything until someone touched her legs. She said she felt the power of the Holy Spirit go all through her body and knew she was healed.

We heard of many miracles of healing at St. Luke's. One Friday night I was wishing that I could participate in one of those healings when suddenly I had a mental picture of being inside the body of a woman being prayed for because she had an ear infection. I could see God's light streaming from the hands on her head into her body and pushing at her ears, but her spirit was unresponsive. I heard mentally words that I said aloud, "The Light is in you. Reach out and touch it for your healing." Her spirit timidly moved toward the Light, and I heard and said, "Praise God, quickly." Everyone sang "Praise God from

Whom All Blessings Flow," and her spirit moved on out with the Light for healing. I learned two or three weeks later that she received a gradual healing which definitely began that night.

One Friday night before the meeting began, I noticed a woman obviously praying to herself. Her body was trembling. As soon as the meeting began, she spoke in tongues. She was repeating the same three or four syllables over and over, and I asked, "Lord, is this for real? How can she be saying anything that makes sense with just those few syllables?" Immediately I had a vivid mental vision of Jesus out in space over the world. Light streamed from His body and swept back and forth over the whole earth. I saw millions of people on earth, but only a few were aware of the light. They looked up and received His blessing. Betty gave the interpretation and described exactly what I had seen.

I was once at a large community meeting in which a woman sang in tongues. I wished to interpret one of those songs sometime. Then God gave me the whole interpretation, but I was terrified to sing it before that big crowd. I have never been given the opportunity again. That gave me a personal lesson in the saying, "Use it or lose it."

Anyone can do what I am learning to do. I am not some great spiritual giant with an unusual gift. I am just an ordinary Christian trying to do what I believe God wants me to do. I believe that God's purpose in having me write this book, if it ever gets published, is to give ordinary Christians the assurance that they can hear from Him and follow His personal guidance. People at my church know me for what I am, just an old lady who sometimes gives a word of prophecy for the encouragement of the body; sometimes interprets a tongue; sometimes has a word of knowledge for someone's encouragement; and sometimes prays with others on our prayer chain or in a small group of intercessors on Saturday night.

We tend to stand in awe of well-known teachers who hold seminars, appear on television, and write books. We think we could never do what they do. I am learning from them, and God is telling me that if I spent as much time in prayer as they do and really made myself available to Him for whatever He wants to do through me, nothing would be impossible. I believe that the secret of hearing from God is believing that He exists

Examples of Hearing God

and recognizing that He created everything and everyone, and has a plan for each part of His creation and for each individual person. He will give us a life of joy and peace if we try to follow His plan.

When we lose our joy and peace, we know it is time to ask God what is blocking the channel to Him. Even small sins can block the way. Is it because I do not trust Him in this problem? Did I fail to do the last thing He told me to do? Did I break one of His commandments? There is a small book, *The Calvary Road,* that explains this beautifully. The gist of the book is that when you lose your joy and peace, the way back is the same way you got on the Calvary Road in the first place. You must confess your sin and commit your life again to obedience to His Lordship.

I believe that I receive answers to my questions when I really trust Him and am determined to follow His instruction, no matter how it may conflict with what I would prefer to do or believe. This is in keeping with James 1:5-9 which tells us that, if we lack wisdom, we are to ask God in faith and not to waver, and that if we are double-minded, we will not get anything from God.

I have had the experience of making life-changing decisions based on my own opinion rather than asking for God's guidance. With hindsight, I know that God is a lot wiser than I am, and I know I would have been better off if I had sought and followed His plan rather than mine. I will give an instance in someone else's life.

I was in a store back in the 1970s and saw a woman from the church I attended then. She was standing several aisles from me looking like she was lost in a mental fog. I went to her and said, "Can I help you? You look like you have a serious problem."

She explained that her husband, "Bob" (not his real name), was an alcoholic. They had a young adopted son, and the Alcoholics Anonymous family support group was urging her to divorce her husband because he was not trying to help himself. I advised her to ask the Lord what to do, rather than do what that group advised. I explained the Scripture referred to above. She said she would do that, and I promised to pray for them.

I saw her at church a week or two later and she said that when she asked God what to do, He said, "Apologize to him." She responded,

"Me apologize to him? He is the one who should be apologizing." But God did not respond.

So she said, "All right, but you will have to tell me what to say because I do not know anything for which I should be apologizing."

She went to the doorway of the bedroom where he sat looking very sad. She felt sorry for him. She went and knelt in front of him and said, "Bob, please forgive me for judging you. I don't have any right to judge you." He started to cry, and she stood up and put her arms around him while they cried together. She then believed that they would work out their problem with God's help.

Chapter 10

God Talks to Everyone

GOD'S HOLY SPIRIT has been here since He participated in the creation of the earth, and He has been talking to everyone who will listen ever since. He inspired every word of the Bible, and He does not contradict Himself. We have to be sure that what we think we hear from God lines up with what He said in the Bible. Long before there was a Bible, people were guided by the Holy Spirit. They would exercise their God-given free wills. If we want to, we can follow our intellectual reasoning and get in trouble as Adam and Eve did when they listened to Satan instead of God.

They ate of the Tree of the Knowledge of Good and Evil. It was, no doubt, a decision to follow the guidance of their intellectual reasoning and thus try to become equal to God. He created them to be His companions in the beautiful world He had created for them to rule under His headship. He wanted their obedience to come by their choice, and so He gave them access to both the Tree of Life and the Tree of the Knowledge of Good and Evil. When they chose to follow Satan and their intellects, He took away access to the Tree of Life. It is now saved in heaven for those who come back to His headship through the blood of Jesus.

Since modern man has the complete Bible, Christians tend to depend on it alone to guide us. We need to study the Bible and be fully aware of its teachings so that we recognize thoughts that contradict the Bible. Our natural inclination is to satisfy our own selfish fleshly desires. However, if we are not fully committed to finding God's will in a situation, the voice we hear in our minds may be our human spirit speaking, or one of Satan's demons. It is very important to learn the difference.

Some people seem to think that God speaks to them continuously. We once had a young man at our church who frequently said, "God told me…" when it was obviously an excuse for selfishness and laziness. We have to be very careful to keep our motives pure and know the Bible well so we can judge whether the words in our minds line up with God's Word.

We can be so deceived by investigating false teachings that we are never willing to receive the truth when it is presented to us. We had a close friend who grew up with a mother who went to a so-called "church" that communicated with what they believed to be the dead. They had many real spiritual experiences that they believed came from God. I tried to help her see the truth, and she corresponded with Father Dennis Bennett, but neither of us could persuade her that those experiences were from demonic sources. She was convinced that reincarnation is God's plan.

Another friend who had investigated all sorts of strange demonic teachings that she mixed with Christianity had a vision in which the sink and everything around her became one shimmering cloud. She heard the words, "Everything is God. You are God." She was convinced that reincarnation is God's plan of salvation, and since she is a part of God, she could, therefore, do anything. I took her to St. Luke's and she spoke of feeling God's presence in a powerful way. She said foreign syllables kept coming into her mind, but she pushed them away. Nothing I said could convince her that it was not God who gave her that vision. She will not read the Bible. She thinks she has the whole truth.

God gave us a conscience to restrain us from sin, and He gives us gentle impressions to check us if we start to do something that could be wrong or dangerous. Sometimes He speaks through words in our minds or through dreams or mental visions. Some people even tell of seeing visions with their eyes or hearing God's voice with their ears. I never have, but I am confident that it can happen because there are instances of these things in the Bible. However, we need to check our dreams and visions against God's book. God may highlight certain verses of Scripture that fit a particular decision we need to make, or He may have someone else say something that gives us an answer without that other person knowing it was God speaking to us. God tries to guide everyone because He "is longsuffering to us-ward, not willing that any should perish, but that all should come to repentance" (2 Pet. 3:9).

Psalm 139 shows us that God knew us before we were born. Hebrews 1:14 tells us about angels who are "ministering spirits, sent forth to minister for them who shall be heirs of salvation." There are numerous passages in the Bible that speak of angels sent to protect people or speak to them.

I first learned about ministering spirits from an experience I had when I was twelve years old. I am sure God guided Aunt Ida to tell me about it because God knew what was going to happen two weeks later. She said, "Dixie, if you ever have a feeling that you should or should not do something, listen to it because it is your guardian angel trying to protect you."

We lived in a small village in Louisiana with just three streets leading to a small business area. We regularly took a shortcut diagonally through some woods between two streets. I went to town one morning for the mail and groceries and was about to step across the gutter and enter that diagonal path when a demanding voice said in my mind, "There is death in the woods."

I thought, *Oh, no. Where did that idea come from? You can see all over the woods. There is nothing in there. If it were a snake, he would run from me when he hears me coming.*

I started to step across the gutter, and God activated in my memory the voice of my sister, Irma, who had died two years before. She was five years my senior and had been a little mother to me, as had my other older sister, Doris. The language was typical of her, "Don't go in there you little fool. Do you want to die?" The hair stood up on the back of my head.

I thought, *Well, I may never know whether this is true or not, but it won't hurt me to follow the road, and at least I will live to tell the tale.*

Sons of God

When I was turning the corner at the top of the hill, I heard a tree fall, but had no idea where it was because I am not good at locating the direction of sounds. The following morning I walked through the woods as usual, and in the middle of the woods, I found a huge rotten tree across the path with crumbled pieces all around it. I remembered yesterday's experience, which I had dismissed as foolishness. I stood in shock as I measured by sight the distance I had traveled to the top of the hill or would have traveled to this spot. I knew that if I had persisted in following my reasoning mind, I would have been crushed by that tree.

Chapter 11

Commitment to God's Plan

I CANNOT REMEMBER any time when I doubted the reality of God or the truth of the Bible. I always expected to have the born-again experience my Baptist teachers talked about. However, I was eighteen before I understood enough to know I had to talk to God about being born-again and commit my life to Him in order to receive new life. After the experience with the fallen tree, I never had any doubts about guardian angels and God's guidance.

I have a cradle roll certificate and I was taken to church and heard sermons on salvation all of my young years, but when the minister said salvation was by faith and instructed that one must repent of sins, I could not understand the road to salvation. Of course I believed it all, but what sins had I ever committed that were bad enough for a loving God to send me to hell?

I was near death at age two and again at age nine, and it was my mother's prayers that saved me both times. After I committed my life to do whatever God wanted, Doris, my oldest sister, told me that my mother had committed my life to God during the illness when I was two. Mother prayed, "If you will save her for me, I will raise her for you." She expected me to be a missionary, but she did not want me to know until after I made a commitment because she did not want me to be influenced by being told about that prayer.

SONS OF GOD

When I was fifteen, a Sunday school teacher predicted that I would be a missionary. I was appalled at the thought, but wondered whether she knew something I did not. I wrestled with the thought that I might be disobedient to God if I refused. When I was nineteen, about a year after I was born-again, a visiting evangelist at Istrouma Baptist Church preached a sermon on the call to missions. With tears streaming, I went forward and committed my life. My pastor sent me to see his wife, my mentor, and on the way across the church grounds, I knew that God had not planned for me to be a missionary. He just wanted me to make a commitment to do whatever He called me to do.

I tried to go to the Baptist Bible Institute thinking I could receive the training necessary for the calling, but every door was closed. Instead, I spent six years in college and wound up with a master of social work degree. I worked for public welfare, then for the Red Cross during World War II. My last job in social work was placing children for adoption and in foster homes, and also supervising some in a temporary institution in Seattle, Washington.

After I learned to listen intently for God to give me the interpretation of tongues and had committed myself to listen for His guidance in prayer instead of just bringing Him my want list, I began to have some unusual experiences. Our Northern Lights prayer meetings were always exciting. I frequently interpreted other people's tongues. One evening, a visitor who doubted the reality of what we were doing was convinced because he said he heard me speaking in Old Flemish, a language he said had been dead for one hundred years, but was the basis for five Germanic languages, all of which he knew.

A couple in the group had a neighborhood problem with a mentally ill woman who was not receiving needed help. We all prayed about it. I would speak in Old Flemish and others would interpret it. God was giving advice about how the situation should be handled.

The doubter would say, "That's what she said. It wasn't in those words, but it was the same idea."

We persuaded him to let us help him receive the baptism in the Holy Spirit. While we were trying to get him to speak, I spoke a few words in Old Flemish, and he said, "I know what you said." I asked what, and he said, "Such a stubborn fool." Some weeks later he did receive

Commitment to God's Plan

and would visit our group when in town. He said he hoped to hear me speak Old Flemish again, but I never did. We told him that God had done something special for him to convince him to receive.

He said that he had tested God a lot before he received. One test was a challenge that if God were truly real, He would stack up some wood perfectly against the outside wall of his house. He turned his back and threw the wood behind him, then turned around, and it was perfectly stacked.

One evening during our Northern Lights meeting, I received a very vivid mental vision with my eyes closed. I saw a brilliant green stem shoot up suddenly. There was a pause, and then a brilliant green leaf shot out. Other pauses and other leaves were added, then a small pink bud. It seemed that I gazed at the bud for a very long time, and suddenly the bud popped open—a big beautiful blossom.

I asked what it meant, and God said that what the world was experiencing right now was the beginning of a big revival of faith in God, but that it was only a small part of what would happen much later. One evening, three of us received mental visions with the same meaning. One man who loved boating saw it as small ships gathering in a harbor, one at a time, a long pause, and then a large gathering suddenly. One woman saw it as a small stream trickling over a bank, a long pause, and then a flood of water. I saw it as a batch of popcorn in a pot, with a few pops now and then, and a sudden popping of the whole pot. God said, "The hot ones pop first."

Most of the time my prayer life has been one of trying to pray according to God's guidance. Occasionally I may have a word of prophecy or a word of knowledge to help someone. This ability was expanded through my trying to help Margaret, a new member of the Northern Lights, by praying for her personal problems. I wished one day that Jane, one of the original members of Northern Lights, was there with us. Just then she called, prayed with us on the telephone, and Jane was added to our weekly morning meetings.

God told us that He had brought the three of us together to teach us how to minister under His direction. We were to greet one another and go immediately to silent prayer until He took charge of the meeting by giving one of us a word of instruction about the prayer topic for the day. Later He was going to add other people from time to time, but we were not to tell anyone about our meetings because He wanted to bring them to us.

After we had been meeting for a few weeks, there came a knock at the door by someone wanting prayer. Others were added from time to time. We ministered to them and taught them what we had been learning. Sometimes there were as many as fifteen, then suddenly we would be back to three.

One woman, Audrey, came doubting the reality of the baptism. She was puzzled because she had been in a meeting her sister took her to and heard tongues in English. Any time someone spoke in tongues, she heard it in English. She called Margaret and asked for help. She and a personal friend of Margaret's were the only ones I knew who had been invited to our meetings. Some of those who came may have told others about us.

Once Audrey said, "I don't understand why you said, 'I would like every one of you to speak in tongues'" (I Cor. 14:5 NIV). She said we were speaking in Polish and those words were in the middle in English. We said that we did not say that, but that God must have said that to her. She eventually received the baptism.

Once several women I did not know came to just one of our meetings. One of them stood next to me in a circle while we prayed. Three times I had a mental picture of putting my hand on her forehead and saying, "The Lord wants to bless you." I resisted because I knew nothing about her. By the third prompting, I realized it had to be an order, so I did it. She burst into tears and said, "On the way over here I told the Lord that if one of you put your hand on my forehead and said, 'The Lord wants to bless you', I would know that He really wants us to move to New Orleans. My husband has been transferred there and I really do not want to leave my home and family here." Suppose I had not obeyed?

There have been a few spectacular experiences. One of the first happened shortly after we received the gift of tongues. I was beginning to try to write my first unpublished book because I felt that the Lord was telling me to develop the writing ability I had longed for. We had bought a very old typewriter in a Navy surplus sale, and it needed a new ribbon. I tried desperately to put the new ribbon in it, but failed.

Commitment to God's Plan

I laid it aside for Stan to install. I had cleared my schedule to have all the next day to write.

The next morning after I was alone, I went to the typewriter and remembered that I had not asked Stan to change the ribbon. In despair I cried out, "God, now what do I do?" I thought about a few miracles I had heard about recently, like cars that ran on empty tanks or with serious problems that should have made them inoperable when someone on an important assignment from God needed to get somewhere.

I sat in front of the typewriter with the ribbon in both hands, shut my eyes, and prayed fervently, "God, this is an emergency if you want me to work on this book today. You know that I am too mechanically stupid to put this ribbon in, so please do it for me." I started speaking in tongues, and God's anointing came on me while my hands moved rapidly on the typewriter. Suddenly I stopped, looked up, and the ribbon was perfectly installed. Now you can believe this or not as you choose, but I know absolutely that it happened.

Another "absolutely happened" experience came also during those early Holy Spirit days. I was in a service in which Wayne Butchart was praying for people and we saw miracles happen. Some were for people with one leg shorter than the other. We watched while the legs grew out. I had been told by a chiropractor years before that my right leg was quite a bit shorter than the left, but I lived in partial denial. After the service was over, I regretted not asking for prayer for the short leg. Every day for six weeks, I prayed that God would allow me to be in another service in which Wayne Butchart ministered so I could ask for his healing touch.

We rarely missed home group meetings, but we did one Wednesday. On Thursday morning at St. Luke's communion and teaching service, a member of the prayer group told me that Wayne Butchart had been at their meeting and two people had their short legs grow out. I was greatly disappointed and cried out to her that I had prayed for six weeks that God would allow me to be where he could pray for my short leg.

She said, "Dixie, you don't need Wayne Butchart to pray for you. Jesus is the healer. You just ask God to make your leg grow out."

I was certain that I did not have that kind of faith, so I just said, "Ha!"

On Saturday morning I was preparing to take a bath and still fuming at God for not letting me be at that meeting. Finally, I said, "OK, if you want to show me that I do not need Wayne Butchart to make my leg grow and I just need to ask Jesus to do it, I will do it."

I sat down in the tub and put my forefinger on my right thigh, shut my eyes, and said, "Leg, in the name of Jesus, grow out to be equal with the other one."

I felt only a slight heat under my finger for a moment then looked at my feet, and my legs were of equal length and have been ever since.

At the next home group meeting everyone was talking about the previous meeting, and one of the men stretched out his legs to show how someone else had his leg lengthened. I saw that his right leg was about two or three inches shorter than the left. I asked whether he knew this. He answered that he did and did not know why he had not asked for prayer. I asked whether he wanted prayer now, and he said that he did.

As soon as I saw that short leg, I knew God had something more to teach me, and that if I prayed for his leg, it would grow out. When I suggested that we pray for him, everyone gathered around him, one man kneeling and holding his feet. They prayed, but the kneeling man kept reporting that there was no growth. Finally, I put my finger on his thigh and commanded, "In the name of Jesus, leg, grow out to be equal with the other."

The kneeling man said, "It's growing! It's growing! Don't pray any more. It's long enough." They were all delighted at what they had accomplished, and no one noticed that it had been my prayer to which the leg had responded. It was all right because God taught me that He is in charge of miracles, and He does them his way. He also uses those He wants to perform each one. The important thing is for us to be sure we listen to Him and obey.

Also during that early time of our Holy Spirit excitement, Jane and her family came on a Sunday afternoon for an unexpected visit to our cabin on Lake Roessiger. They had brought dinner for all of us. After we ate, everyone was enjoying activities on the lake. Jane asked me to go into the cabin with her and ushered me into our bedroom.

Commitment to God's Plan

She said, "I am going to show you something, and I want you to pray for me and not tell anyone else. The others would tell me to go to the doctor, but you have faith to believe God for a healing."

She showed me a large dark mole on her back. I became alarmed. I described to her having seen in a large glass case in a lab at college, a mole and all the growth behind it. I urged her to go to her doctor and have it removed before it started to grow.

She said emphatically, "No! You are going to pray for it, and it is going to go away!"

Nothing I said made her budge, so I silently prayed, "God, please help me. You have to say this prayer, because I do not know what to do with her."

I put my forefinger on the mole, closed my eyes, and prayed in tongues while that mole jumped up and down under my finger. She reported later that it hurt so much she wanted to scream. I felt a powerful anointing all the time, and when the interpretation came I was listening so intently that I did not realize what I was saying until I finished, "No matter what you see, and no matter what you feel, keep praising my name for the healing that is taking place right now."

Immediately I started begging her to go to the doctor, but she said, "No! He said...", and she quoted me exactly. For the next three months she reported to me that the mole was growing and becoming more painful. I continued to beg her to see her doctor. Each time she quoted what "He said..."

Finally, one day she said, "Dixie, you know that mole you prayed for?" I started my plea. She said, "It's gone."

She showed me her back, and there was no sign that there had ever been a mole there. The only way I can explain it is that Jane's faith and God's plan took care of the mole. I had nothing to do with it. I was only a very unwilling participant. God must have caused the mole to pull the inside growth to the outside of her body and then drop off.

Another spectacular experience happened at the end of the Vietnam War. Every night around 2 AM during the week when we were evacuating Vietnam, I woke up with the impression that God had a prayer request. I would go into the living room and say, "All right, Lord, what is it you want me to pray about?" I would then speak in tongues for a while and then in English, always about something I had no way of knowing about. The next morning I would go into the kitchen, never aware of it being any particular time, turn on the radio, and hear the announcement that what I had prayed for, word for word as I had prayed it, was happening.

One night I prayed for the missionaries to go down from the mountains to the coast to try to get ship passage out. I did not know there were missionaries still in Vietnam, did not even know there were mountains in Vietnam. The next morning the first words I heard were, "The missionaries have decided to go down out of the mountains, etc." as I had prayed.

One night I prayed for people to get small boats and go out to any ships they could get on. Another night I prayed that our Navy would send ships to pick up anyone who wanted to leave Vietnam. Another night I prayed for people to go up to the tops of buildings and have helicopters pick them off and take them to ships.

I believe that it was about 1980 when Israel found out that Russia had been shipping war supplies in submarines and storing them in specially made tunnels in Lebanon, preparing for a surprise attack on Israel. For a month before that discovery was made, God had me praying every day for Israel to find that stuff and haul it out. I could see mental pictures of the digging of those tunnels, the submarines coming in and unloading the war materials, tanks, trucks, etc. into the tunnels at the edge of the water. I kept thinking that I must be imagining this. I kept praying as directed, and no one was more surprised than I was when the news came on the air describing things exactly as I had seen them. God must have had a lot of people praying for that discovery. I cannot believe that it was my prayers alone that led to it. Many probably prayed in tongues without ever knowing what they were praying for.

Chapter 12

The Prayer of Commitment

THERE WAS ONE unusual experience, around 1933 or 1934, when my sister Doris was living on the farm on which her husband Aubrey and his siblings had grown up. His sister, Eula, and her husband, our Uncle Arch, and their four children were there also during the depression. I was in my bedroom one morning when a thought flashed through my mind, "Doris is dying!" I wondered where that idea came from, but I realized that things like that could be real. I knelt by my bed and prayed as though I knew it was true. I had looked at the clock when the thought came and knew it was eleven o'clock. I had heard that when you pray in a crisis for someone very close to you, you must be ready to make the sacrifice that Abraham did when he was ready to offer up his son Isaac.

Therefore, I prayed, "Lord, you know how important Doris is to me. She has been like a beloved mother all of my life, and I cannot imagine being without her. You know that I want her to live, but, if you can glorify your name more by taking her than you can by letting her live now, I want your will to be done."

I set aside clothes and other things that I could quickly pack if I were called to go to her. At one o'clock, a neighbor called me to their telephone. We did not have a telephone. On the way to the neighbor's I thought, *Will the person calling say, "Doris is dying," or "Doris is dead"? If he says, "Doris is dying," I will know that she will live.*

SONS OF GOD

A stranger who answered the phone said, "Doris is dying, and your family wants you to come at once."

I received this as welcome news. The neighbor took me to Doris, and I found that she was recovering and had sent for a doctor. Aunt Eula explained that she and Luther, her teenaged son, had been consulting with Doris about work she wanted Luther to do for her when Doris had a sudden sinking spell. She sent Luther to call a doctor and have someone call me. Aunt Eula said that when she saw this sinking spell she thought, *Doris is dying*.

I asked what time this happened and Aunt Eula said, "It was eleven o'clock. I looked at the clock."

Another instance of the prayer of commitment for a loved one came to my nephew, Leon. In 1973, my brother Reynolds was dying from cancer of the lungs because of his lifelong smoking habit. He started smoking when he was a young child and always had too much money available. He finally had almost no lungs with which to breathe. He gave up smoking two weeks before his death only because he could no longer stand it.

His son, Leon, called me from Grove, Oklahoma, to pray for him. We had many long conversations in which I encouraged him to believe in a healing. I had heard of so many great miracles, I knew God could heal him if He chose. Leon called many others to pray also. When time passed without a healing, it finally occurred to me that God did not plan to heal him.

I prayed, "Lord, I know you can heal him. How can we receive a healing? Are you going to heal him?"

He said, "Reynolds made the decision that is destroying his lungs. I am not going to take away the consequences of that decision."

I asked, "Then what am I going to tell Leon? I have been encouraging him to believe in a healing."

He said, "Tell him of your experience when you thought Doris was dying. He must be willing to give up his father before I can work in this situation."

I told Leon, and he and his father both committed their wills to God for whatever would bring glory to God. Reynolds died very quickly with Leon and Marie (Reynold's wife) at his side.

The Prayer of Commitment

Leon had indirectly led his parents to receive Jesus as Lord and Savior when he was a child. When he was four, he had insisted that they take him to church. Reynolds had said, "I guess he's going to be another one of those praying Vernons."

Reynolds knew about miraculous healing. When he was a teenager, he lost an eye when a wire tore his eyeball open. The doctor was going to remove the eyeball the following morning. His father called for the elders of their church to anoint him with oil and pray for healing (see James 5:14-15). When the doctor removed the bandage the next morning, the eye was totally restored. However, that eye was stony for the rest of his life.

Reynolds finally received his born-again experience after an angelic visitation in which he had an experience like Paul's on the road to Damascus (see Acts 9). He learned to love the Lord and even taught in Sunday school.

He and Leon had the usual Baptist attitude toward speaking in tongues, but Reynolds had made one attempt to receive about two years before this. Because of my talking so much to Leon and sending him books on the subject, Leon received the baptism in the Holy Ghost and led friends and relatives to receive. They had a prayer group of fifteen, including the pastor, in his church. The church invited them to leave.

The pastor found another church, and the prayer group formed a church of their own and asked Leon to be their pastor. He worked full-time and acted as a pastor part-time until the church grew large enough to support his ministry. Their church is named, "Grove Christian Center."

While they were struggling to build their church in their little resort city, of Grove, Oklahoma, Leon and Lynda would go to the resorts on the lakes and minister before church time. Sometimes they stood on a platform on the main highway in town and Lynda would sing until a group of cars stopped. Then Leon would preach to them. Thus his father's death brought glory to God by getting Leon into the ministry God had called him to during his youth. He and Lynda married as soon as they graduated from high school. They had four daughters within the first few years of their marriage. He was kept busy earning a living and had no time to consider a full-time ministry or training for one.

He has trained himself by studying the Bible and believing what it says. He reads books by others who lived close to the Lord. Thus, he has missed being confused by all the liberalism that has crept into the modern seminaries. Many people have experienced miracles and deliverance through his ministry.

Many pastors come to him for teaching, and he holds seminars and conferences and goes as a missionary to foreign countries. His church sends out missionaries to Central America, Eastern Europe, South Africa, and the Far East. Their children and grandchildren are all working for the Lord. Three of their daughters and their husbands are missionaries.

Lynda goes alone or with Leon on short missionary trips. She ministers in ladies meetings, Aglow, and churches. Her ministry is sought after because she flows freely in the gifts of the Spirit. She has a beautiful voice that has added a lot to their ministry. She has made many albums of her music. In addition, she has been a very wise wife, mother, and grandmother. In response to my request, Leon wrote the following about their ministry.

> Pray for us! When others are slowing down, our schedule becomes more intense. If I go on half the mission trips that have opened this year, I will be gone more than last year. Several very large ministries in Africa want me to come and teach leaders. Nepal needs minister training. Also, China invitations have been extended. Russia, Central America, and the Philippines are always requesting that I come to them. God still has not released me from pastoring this church, so I need wisdom and more gifted ministers to share the ministry.
>
> The need I see in the mission churches and leaders are: (1) teaching on spirit, soul, and body; (2) the gifts of the Holy Ghost, especially the gift of prophecy; (3) Spiritual authority and commitment; (4) family. I have spent several years teaching on knowing God and listening to His Voice.
>
> I will write a little about our beginning at Daddy's sickness and death.
>
> Some people that we meet are often classified as different or strange because they do not meet a 'normal' standard. Many years ago,

The Prayer of Commitment

my aunt Dixie was in that category. She talked about experiencing hearing God and talking to him in a strange language. You see, we were Southern Baptists and we did not talk about hearing God. We prayed, but evidently, did not listen. Our church taught that praying in tongues was not for today.

In January of 1973, my daddy found out that he had lung cancer after fifty-two years of smoking and thirty years of refinery work. He loved God and was my spiritual father as well as my daddy. In his last three weeks, we spent a lot of time talking and praying. He shared that he had sought for the Holy Ghost while living in Texas in 1969 and 1970. We called everyone asking for prayer. One of those I called was my dad's sister, Aunt Dixie. I knew she would pray and seek God. She also sent me books about the Holy Ghost and prayer.

During my daddy's short sickness, I surrendered to the call to preach. (I had been called eighteen years earlier.) I was filled with the Holy Ghost twenty-four days after my dad's death, and was slain in the Spirit. I became one of the "different and strange" Christians.

The Fire of God swept through our church, baptizing about twelve or fourteen people. We began meeting for prayer in homes, and hundreds were saved, filled, and healed in a few months. We preached on the streets, in homes and resorts, and attended every meeting in our area where the Holy Ghost might be. Normally, if we went, the Holy Ghost was always manifesting.

Since we became "strange and different," our small group has started churches and Bible schools all over the world. Our local church is not a mega-church, but we serve a mighty God. Millions have been changed, and the story is still in action.

My aunt Dixie sought God, listened to his voice, and shared her love and faith. She did not travel to the mission fields, but her faith and seed is still producing daily.

Chapter 13

Is It Really You, God?

IN SPITE OF the fact that I have had these (to me) spectacular experiences in hearing from God, I am very cautious about claiming that things which seem to be from God really are. I have sometimes kept a record of things that I thought I had received from God in prayer. In going over them, I see that not everything could have been from God. My own imagination and observance of things going on in the world no doubt influenced my messages. It seems to me that the only way we can be sure that God told us about something that is going to happen is to wait and see if it really does.

The surest things I have received have been based on something I picked up in the spiritual world that was actually happening or being planned by someone or some group of people. God may tell us about some future event, like my being told about meeting Agnes Sanford. This knowledge was obviously given for my encouragement. God does not speak to us about all that happens in our lives, and does not give direct instruction for all that we do. We have to live by faith and be aware of His presence. We should notice if our peace departs over something we are planning to do, then pray about it before proceeding. I believe that God has told me not to worry about this, but keep believing that He does speak to me, and as I put my trust in His word to me I will be able to receive more accurately and thereby be guided.

Sons of God

Margaret said recently that she has noticed that the so-called great modern prophets—who meet annually and try to find out from God what will happen—usually miss what really happens such as hurricanes, volcanoes, earthquakes, and wars, and what they predict usually does not happen. They certainly did not predict what happened on September 11, 2001. There must have been some who had a feeling that something terrible was about to happen.

I personally remember that for two weeks before the terrible Oklahoma bombing I had a strong feeling of impending disaster and sorrow over something that would affect the lives of many. I mentioned this to Ed Allen just a few days before it happened, and he said he had the same feeling. Ed Allen, with his Storehouse Ministries, was a member of our church for several years until he was required to start a church of his own in order for people to receive tax deductions for their contributions to his work in the Soviet Union and Central America. He frequently had part-time schools that trained for missionary and personal ministry work. Before and after he started his own church, he also had what he called "Monday Night Holy Spirit Meetings" to train attendees in how to hear the Holy Spirit in ministry. I attended these meetings until he moved to Texas. The morning of the Oklahoma bombing, when I heard it on the news, I called his house to tell him that this was it. For months before the September 11 bombings, I believe many of us had a feeling that we would soon experience some major disaster. If only we could live close enough to the Lord for him to show us a disaster about to happen so we could do something to prevent it.

Most prophecy in church services is really just an encouragement from the Lord or an admonition to keep pressing in to a closer relationship and obedience to His guidance. Sometimes He seems to be giving more direct instruction to help in our growth or to help us carry out His plan. God is not a fortune-teller. He occasionally gives us a brief glimpse of the future when it helps Him prepare us for it.

I have sometimes noticed that the teaching on several different radio or TV programs have similar messages, which seem to indicate that different spiritual leaders are hearing from God about what He wants taught at that time. In the last few years, He has seemed to guide pastors from different churches in given communities to get together regularly for prayer for revival. There is a general feeling now that we are moving toward the greatest revival in world history.

Some messages that I have received over the last few years have warned that very hard times are coming, both in economic problems and natural disasters. He keeps saying that He must allow these things to happen because very few people will turn to Him when they have only a few problems. When the crisis arrives, most people will cry out to God for help. We must keep close to Him and learn to hear His voice so that we are able to bring in the final harvest of souls that will be ready for reaping when disasters multiply. If we do not prepare now with much prayer and Bible study for these national and worldwide trials, we will be hurt like the rest of the world. If we are close to Him and able to hear His voice accurately, He will protect us. Our very lives may depend upon it.

We have to remember that Jesus said the wheat and the tares will ripen together. Other Scriptures tell us that the evil and the good will become increasingly worse or increasingly better. Therefore, Christians should expect that the more our lights shine and the more souls we win to Christ, the more persecution we can expect from those who are too stubbornly committed to evil to repent. As individuals and nations fall more into sin, God withdraws His presence and blessing to allow them to reap the consequences of opening the door to Satan, whose purpose is "to steal, kill and destroy" (John 10:10). Natural disasters increase and favorable weather for crops and pleasant living conditions decrease where Satan is active. We must draw closer to God and to each other in order to survive in this final harvest of the saved and the unsaved.

During the week before Cheryl Schang's visit in November 2001, I heard a program on TBN when a Christian auditor spoke of his ministry to Christians about their financial problems. The host asked him whether he believed we were going into several years of hard times financially, and he said, "Absolutely. Without a doubt."

That night I dreamed I was a few miles from home in North King County, walking in strange neighborhoods and trying to find a street I knew would take me to my home in Mountlake Terrace. I knew I was walking northward, but nothing looked familiar. Every house and business building was in a terrible state of decay, and the people all looked sad and discouraged.

Finally, I came to a cliff with a steep drop-off, and below was a beautiful field with a lush crop. A farmer using a horse-drawn vehicle was gathering a bountiful harvest. My spirits lifted and I started to praise God, "Oh, Lord, everything you create is so very beautiful, and everything that man makes just decays to dust."

I woke up and wondered whether this was a prophetic dream or whether I just had the dream because of what I had heard on the TV program. During one of Cheryl's teaching periods she spoke of prophetic dreams, and I told her of this dream and asked whether it was prophetic. She said that it was and that God was telling me that we are going to have some years of financial decline, but that those who trust in God will be taken care of. She said that it was like the account of Isaac's experience in the twenty-sixth chapter of Genesis. There was a famine in the land, but Isaac planted a field and reaped a hundred-fold crop.

I believe that God tries to protect and guide everyone who will listen. This certainly seems to be indicated by what happened in the terrorist attacks on the World Trade Center and the Pentagon on September 11, 2001. Only about one-quarter of the tickets that were sold and scheduled for the four commercial planes used in those bombing attacks were used. Could there have been even fewer people on those planes if others had listened to the still small voice telling them not to fly that day? There were many stories about people who, for some reason, did not go to work or visit the World Trade Center buildings that morning, or who miraculously escaped. Could God have saved more if they had been listening to Him?

We should certainly pray for the terrorists who attacked us, and for those who plan to attack us, because we never know which of them could have an experience as Paul did on the road to Damascus and become our most helpful friends in getting the terrorism stopped. No matter how evil they are, God has said, "Whosoever shall call upon the name of the Lord shall be saved" (Rom. 10:13). At the same time, we need to pray for guidance in using our governmental authorities and military and policing organizations, which God said He established for our protection and to punish evildoers (see Rom. 13:1-4).

Is It Really You, God?

We certainly need to pray for the moral reform of our government. Our nation as a whole has sunk so deep in sin that the lawmakers and courts and administrative directives all over the country have tended to embrace the protection of gross sin and put those who embrace God's principles in jeopardy. Could the terrorist attacks and the present depression be the beginning of our nation reaping the consequences?

I asked God several times recently who is right: those who believe that Christians will be raptured before the final seven years of tribulation, or those who believe that we will have to live through all or part of it. He finally answered that it does not matter which argument wins. What matters is that all of us should understand that, regardless of when He comes for us, we are going to live through some very hard times, harder than anything we have ever seen on this earth, and we should be preparing ourselves spiritually now for the hard times that have already started and will get much worse.

I personally wish that the pre-tribulation teachers are right, but I cannot see it in Scripture because the very Scriptures that they quote to prove it do not fit their interpretation. The whole book of Revelation is about what Jesus told John would happen in these final years. Jesus gave messages to John to give the seven churches. Then in Revelation 4:1, John said that a voice said "Come up hither, and I will shew thee things which must be hereafter." This plainly says that John was to come up, not the churches. Yet some teachers claim that this is the point at which Jesus takes the church to heaven.

They wrongly use 2 Thessalonians 2:6-8 to try to prove that the Holy Spirit is removed with the church when the church is taken to heaven, and that allows the Antichrist to be revealed. However, it is my opinion that this only tells us that he is being prevented from being revealed until his proper time comes and then the Holy Spirit will step out of the way and allow him to have his way. That teaching ignores the previous passage, verses 1-4, which tells us not to expect the rapture until after the coming of the Antichrist. If the Holy Spirit disappeared with the church before the great tribulation, how would anyone else be saved? No one can come to the Father unless the Holy Spirit draws him, and we know that many will be saved during that time.

Jesus said that only the Father knows when the end time events will happen, but He did know that Christians will see the days of the Antichrist because He told his apostles that when they (or a later generation of Christians?) saw him standing in the temple, they should flee to the mountains fast because things were going to be worse than they had ever seen (see Matt. 24:15-22).

Chapter 14

Learning from the Past

SOME OF OUR modern teachers seem to encourage us to believe that any Christian can be showered with material blessings if he gives enough to God's work, but I do not believe that is what God is telling me. When I meditated on the possibility that we will go through another deep depression, God reminded me that He took care of all of our family during the first deep depression. We were tithing and giving offerings, but we had to live through some very hard times financially. He reminded me that I always had a warm house to live in and enough food and clothes, even though toward the end of my senior year in high school I had to put cardboard in my shoes to cover the holes.

Based on all I have learned since those depression days, I realize now that I could have had a new pair of shoes if I had asked God to provide them, because this was really a necessity. James 4:2 says, "Ye have not, because ye ask not." It never occurred to me to ask God for shoes. I had taken a year's leave from my job as a telephone operator in order to finish high school, and the little cash that I had was used up early in that school year. I did not let my family know that I needed shoes because I knew they would feel obligated to buy them, and this was my own responsibility.

James 4:3 warns us that we must not be greedy in our requests, "Ye ask, and receive not, because ye ask amiss, that ye may consume it upon your lusts [or pleasures]." One of the original prayer group members at St. Luke's told me an illustration of this verse. She said she asked the Lord for a new dress for a Christmas party, and He provided it. She was so thrilled that she asked for another dress for the New Year's Eve party, and the Lord said, "I have already given you a dress for your parties."

Aubrey, my sister Doris's husband, was laid off that spring of 1932 in a large reduction of employees at Standard Oil. It was only a few weeks after Doris and Aubrey had adopted a beautiful baby girl who was a delight to all of us. Aubrey's sister, Mary, had called from Texas a few months before Aubrey lost his job to say that she could no longer find work as a nurse and was almost out of money. She had enough for bus fare to Baton Rouge, and so she became my roommate. Now, with Aubrey out of work, there were five of us living without support. Doris told me to go to the store and get boxes for packing because we would have to move to the farm on which Aubrey and his siblings grew up, which was about ninety miles from our rented house in Baton Rouge.

About a year before that, our Uncle Arch, who was married to Aubrey's sister Eula, had been laid off in a big Standard Oil reduction of employees, and they and their four children had moved to the old farm. Doris and Aubrey spent every weekend visiting them, taking a week's supply of food until Uncle Arch and his two boys could begin earning money from cash crops.

On my way to the store, I went to the parsonage and cried out my distress to my Sunday school teacher, Mrs. Buckley. She assured me God would provide for us, and she prayed a very fervent prayer for our provision. The next morning Aubrey received a telephone call telling him that they were putting him on the extra board where he would be earning approximately $60.00 per month painting tanks if it did not rain.

Shortly before graduation, I had to have an appendectomy at the New Orleans Charity Hospital. (It must have been a student who operated because the incision was very long.) It took months for me to regain my strength. By studying at home, I was able to pass the tests, and I graduated from high school at last in May, 1932.

Because I was still weak from the operation and had no money to buy a long white dress, white shoes, and a big bouquet of red roses,

Learning from the Past

I asked the principal to excuse me from the graduation, but did not mention my poverty. The following day, our pastor came to see me with a message from the teachers and principal. They had been crushed over my wanting to skip graduation and had appealed to my pastor to persuade me. When he explained that I could not afford it, they took up a collection among themselves to purchase shoes and roses and arranged for a borrowed dress.

I cried because I was so humiliated, preferring just to slip away from the whole thing with my diploma issued in private. My pastor told me that I would have to learn to receive as well as give. Those teachers and the principal had been delighted to do this for me, and I should be gracious enough to allow them the joy of giving. I followed his advice and felt that I really had learned a new lesson.

I remembered that it had been through tithing that I had my first experience of being aware of the presence of the Lord and had finally been born-again. I had to quit school in 1928 after I finished ninth grade, and I went to work as a cashier in a department store in New Orleans. I was going to church and trying to understand how to receive a born-again experience that Southern Baptists talked about. Preachers thought they explained it clearly, but it rolled over me. When they said just believe and repent of your sins and ask God to forgive you, I would think, *Believe? Of course I believe in God, but sins? What have I done? Of course I have done a few little things I shouldn't have, but God would not send me to hell for eternity for little things like that!*

That fall, a minister preached a sermon on tithing and quoted Malachi 3:10, "Bring ye all the tithes into the storehouse, that there may be meat in mine house, and prove me now herewith, saith the LORD of hosts, if I will not open you the windows of heaven, and pour you out a blessing, that there shall not be room enough to receive it."

I thought, *Well, I do not understand their sermons on faith and repentance, but I do know what a tenth of eight dollars a week is, so I will tithe my income and see how God works to help me get that born again experience.*

I went faithfully to church to give my tenth. I saved it up if I missed a few Sundays. Then I prodded myself to go to church again before I was tempted to spend my tithe. I kept waiting for those promised blessings, thinking all the time that the tithe would go a long way toward buying a new dress, which at that time cost at least fifteen dollars. There was no way I could pay the two dollars per week tuition to night business school, tithe, and buy a dress also. Finally, I decided that tithing was what I ought to do and that I would do it even if I never got a blessing for giving.

Very shortly after I made that decision, my sister Doris came home from work and put a large dress box from a store in my hands and said, "My boss said these dresses were given to her to give to someone who needed them, and she was sure they would fit you."

I opened the box and found a large supply of dresses suitable for all seasons. God became very real to me because I knew that only He had known of my tithing and my complete relinquishment of the consequences to Him.

I continued my search for that born-again experience by reading tracts that I picked up out of a box at the back of the church. Finally, I found one that met my need. It was based on Isaiah 53:6. "All we like sheep have gone astray; we have turned every one to his own way; and the LORD hath laid on him the iniquity of us all." I knew that I had stubbornly wanted my own way many times and had never thought to ask God to tell me what His way was for Me. I saw this as sin worthy of His rejection.

After thinking this over for a few days, I knelt and talked to Him about it. I had a mental vision of Jesus dying on the cross for my sins and heard His words, "And I, if I be lifted up from the earth, will draw all men unto me" (John 12:32). I understood that Jesus had been lifted up on the cross to die for my sins, and He wanted me to lift Him up in my life so that He, through me, could draw others to Him. I asked His forgiveness for all my sins and committed myself to seek His will. I told Him I wanted to lift up Jesus in my life. I was enveloped in His love and knew that I had truly been born-again.

After my high school graduation, I failed to get my job back at the telephone company, and when I tried to apply elsewhere, people would look at me and say, "Don't you know there aren't any jobs?"

About this time Aubrey was put to work on an oil tanker for $60.00 per month. We moved to the family farm to join the family already there. Doris and Aubrey continued to accept a responsibility for anyone in need.

Right after the big Standard Oil layoff that left Uncle Arch without a job, we started getting unexpected visitors: men knocking on the back door asking for food. They were out of work and roaming all over the country on freight trains looking for work. Aubrey told Doris that he did not want her ever to turn any of them away. She was to take them in and fix them the kind of meal she would want if she were hungry. He said, "As long as I have anything, nobody is going to go without food if I can help him." She followed the instructions and I saw Aubrey many mornings frying bacon and eggs for visitor after visitor, sometimes as many as six for breakfast. Aubrey cheered them up with his Will-Rogers-type jokes about our fumbling government trying to deal with this crisis.

The old farmhouse had two very large bedrooms on either side of a very wide hallway open at each end, with a large kitchen behind the two rooms on one side. Uncle Arch's family used the side with the kitchen. Their teenaged son, Luther, built us another kitchen on the other side with me acting as his helper. The well in the yard with a wind-up rope on a bucket was our water supply.

Our transportation was Doris's old Chevrolet coupe for three. She noticed that the farming families on our road had no motorized transportation and no way to get to church or to town to pick up the surplus commodities that finally became available after the public screamed at the government enough to stop them from throwing good food in the river when there were starving people in need. At first we just received flour, but gradually other commodities were added.

Doris was able to buy a big flatbed truck for ten dollars, and Luther applied his natural skills with machinery to repair it. On Sundays and on surplus commodity days he would drive down the road honking the horn and people would come out and climb on the truck for a ride to church or town. They called the truck the "Hootin' Annie." There were no telephones to warn them of his coming.

That was a bleak summer for all of us. Most of the farmers, like Uncle Arch, were so eager to earn money that they planted cash crops that did not sell and they had no vegetable gardens. We were without vegetables for so long that we were delighted when we heard you could cook very small yam leaves for a vegetable. Aunt Eula and I picked the leaves and cooked them with high expectations. They tasted terrible, but we ate them this one time because we were so hungry for vegetables. We ate a lot of beans and rice that summer. Some people in the area had potatoes, but no money to buy anything else. Here was another case of, "Ye have not, because ye ask not" (James 4:2). I am sure some of us, perhaps most, were saying brief bedtime prayers about our (to us) hopeless situation. It never occurred to any of us to get together and seriously seek God's will and have faith that He would hear and answer our request for his guidance and help (see James 4:2). Instead, we leaned on our own understanding. Proverbs 3:5 warns us to trust in God and lean not on our own understanding.

James 1:5-8 teaches us how to find God's best solution for all of our problems. "If any of you lack wisdom, let him ask of God, that giveth to all men liberally, and upbraideth not; and it shall be given him. But let him ask in faith, nothing wavering. For he that wavereth is like a wave of the sea driven with the wind and tossed. For let not that man think that he shall receive anything of the Lord. A double minded man is unstable in all his ways."

God is willing to give wisdom to *anyone* if he asks in faith without any wishy-washy thinking such as, "I'll do it if I think it will work the way I want it to." I have had a few critical situations in which I had to make a decision right away and have cried out silently to God for His guidance, fully intending to do exactly what He wanted me to, even if it was something I really did not want to do. He has always answered me right then with the words to say and the thing to do. His word always turned out to be *wisdom*.

That fall, an old neighbor of ours in Baton Rouge got word to me that the chief operator wanted me to know they would take me back, and the neighbor offered me room and board for $5.00 per week. About two years later, Aubrey got his old job back, and during that interval, Mary was able to find civil service work in a Veteran's Hospital. World War II put Uncle Arch back to work as a machinist.

I believe that what God is showing me is that He cannot trust every believer with a lot of money and luxuries because some would use them selfishly and fall away from Him. Jesus understands our problems because

LEARNING FROM THE PAST

He had the same kind of problems that we do. We understand other people's needs and want to help them because we have lived through similar trials. They are impressed by our faith when they see us joyful in the Lord while we struggle with the same problems that they do. I have experienced both good times and times of poverty, but I believe that both have been God's way of teaching me what Paul said he had learned, how to trust God in all circumstances (see Phil. 4:11-12).

It seems to me that the greatest ministries are those in which the leaders are aware of the fact that they are totally and daily dependent upon God for each day's needs. George Mueller is an outstanding example. If God had given him a year's supply of money to take care of those orphans, would he have been such a man of prayer as he was? He had to pray in every day's supplies, and God always met their needs. He never sent out expensive appeals to long lists of possible contributors. I prefer to give to those ministries that appear to be praying in their needs, and not spending the little I can give pressuring me for more with expensive colorful frequent requests. I do give to some that send the colorful explanations of their ministries when I am convinced that they are reaching multitudes of souls for salvation and ministry.

Chapter 15

Recent Events

ABOUT 1985, THE LORD led Stan and me to join Cornerstone Community Church in Mountlake Terrace, about five years after we moved there from North Seattle. We were very pleased with this church because they spent more time and energy on missions than they did on their local church. With around one hundred families, it was amazing to see the many outreach programs and groups or couples going into either short-term or long-term missionary work. For several years, George Otis, Jr. and his wife, Lisa, and their children have been members of this church. The children go to our church school. They started the Sentinel Group in Lynnwood, Washington, to investigate the geographical areas where the strongholds of Satan have been broken and communities have been transformed by the movement of the Holy Spirit. They have made videos of several of these movements. George travels to many places to show the videos and give advice on how to break Satan's strongholds. I will say more about them in connection with trying to break the strongholds that affect our community.

My experiences in the Ed Allen "Monday Night Holy Spirit Meetings" encouraged me to believe that I was really hearing from God when I ministered to people. I once saw a mental picture of a goat's head over the head of a woman who was being prayed for, and I heard mentally, "Is there a stubborn spirit here?" I learned from Ed later that this was correct.

SONS OF GOD

Another time I saw a dark cloud over a small area in the congregation and realized that God was showing me that someone there needed exorcism from a spirit interfering with the meeting. I stood up and pointed to the area and suggested that someone there needed prayer. No one volunteered. I learned later that the man I suspected was from a church that did not approve of speaking in tongues, and he was there apparently to pray against us. He had been coming regularly, but never came to the meetings again after that time.

One evening Ed told us to ask God what Jesus' reaction was when a saved person arrived in heaven. I had a vision of Jesus taking our deceased daughter, Colleen, in His arms and looking up to the Father to thank Him for giving her to Him. He then looked at me and said, "You can stop praying for her now. She is all right." Since she died in 1983, I had been praying for her progress in heaven because I felt that she still had so much to learn.

Our church and others in the Puget Sound area are still engaged in much prayer in small groups, and we also pray individually for a transforming revival to come to our area. Pastors meet together to pray for this, and to look for the fulfillment of some prophecies that encourage us to believe we will see this in the Puget Sound—especially in our area. I hoped that Cheryl's coming again in January would help bring this to pass.

For several years, the Lord has been telling me that we are going to experience increasingly hard times in many ways, and that at the same time we will bring in the final harvest of souls before the return of Christ. He said that hard times are necessary in order to lead people to cry out to Him for guidance. Those who do not turn to Him will become bitter against Him and against those who believe in Him, so we can expect persecution. It is important for us to draw close to Him and listen for His guidance so that He can keep us safe and functioning in our part in bringing in the final harvest.

About two or three years ago, I was praying both in English and in tongues, and off to one side I saw a vision of four bears standing shoulder to shoulder in a semicircle taking turns licking each other's faces. Finally, I stopped praying and asked, "God, why am I watching a bunch of bears licking each other?"

Recent Events

He said, "It's a bear market. They are propping each other up, but it's still a bear market."

This bear market had nothing to do with the subject of my prayer, so I had to believe that it was really God telling me something. I remembered that some months after we came close to having a market crash in 1997, a financial leader praised some billionaire for saving the stock market by buying a lot of stock and thus restoring public confidence. So it seems that those with the most money can often determine whether the market goes up or down. They can agree among themselves how to influence the small investor. However, behind all that is God influencing them and others, whether they are aware of it or not. God's primary purpose is to save as many souls as He can. So if He wants to put us in deep depression in order to drive us to our knees, He will.

On April 22, 1997, while speaking in tongues, I received a vision of a very large man riding a small donkey. The donkey was happily running as fast as his little legs could travel. I asked, "God, what does this mean? Why is this big man riding such a small animal, and why is he making the donkey go so fast?"

God told me that through the centuries, since the Holy Spirit was given, getting the church to evangelize the world has been like trying to train a dumb, stubborn donkey. Now that He has his donkey beginning to go in the right direction, God is going to do a quick work of getting His message out to the whole world.

Jesus told his disciples, "This gospel of the kingdom shall be preached in all the world for a witness unto all nations; and then shall the end come" (Matt. 24:14). It seems that every generation of Christians has questioned whether it could be that Jesus would come in their generation. Is it possible that He would have come many centuries ago if only His followers had carried out the great commission of making the bringing in of His kingdom their foremost goal, rather than begging Him to bring in their individual kingdoms? Only the Father knows when Jesus will come because only He knew from the beginning which generation would actually get the job done.

The population of the earth keeps multiplying, and the ratio of believers to those who have never heard has not varied much. Therefore, the number of people who have gone to hell without even hearing the gospel message of salvation has multiplied. There are now four billion people in the world who have never heard the name of Jesus. Only recently has the proportion of believers to unbelievers been more encouraging. We now have one believer in every five persons in the world, and the third world countries are producing many evangelists.

God surely will hold each generation responsible for not getting the gospel to everyone. Ezekiel 33:8-9 tells us, "When I say unto the wicked, O wicked man, thou shalt surely die; if thou dost not speak to warn the wicked from his way, that wicked man shall die in his iniquity; but his blood will I require at thine hand. Nevertheless, if thou warn the wicked of his way to turn from it; if he do not turn from his way, he shall die in his iniquity; but thou hast delivered thy soul."

I believe that God is saying to this generation that we have no excuse for failing to get the gospel to everyone in the world because He has given us so much modern technology that we have many ways to reach them. God is also multiplying the miracles to astonish the unbelievers, and His Holy Spirit is pleading with multitudes so that we have an enormous harvest ready to be gathered.

CHAPTER 16

TRUSTING GOD

ONLY LATELY HAVE I begun to understand why God commanded me to "live in joy" when I received the Baptism in the Holy Spirit. Joy and peace are the result of trusting God. Isaiah 26:3 says, "Thou wilt keep him in perfect peace, whose mind is stayed on thee: because he trusted in thee." "The joy of the LORD is your strength" (Neh. 8:10). "In thy presence is fullness of joy" (Ps. 16:11). "The kingdom of God is not meat and drink; but righteousness, and peace, and joy" (Rom. 14:17). John 15 tells of Jesus instructing His followers how to abide in God's love and peace and receive His protection. Psalm 91 tells of the perfect protection that a believer can have if he will abide in that secret place of the Most High. Abide means to live there always, and we do that by obeying His commands and trusting Him implicitly.

After my husband's massive stroke on January 30, 1996, I was able to trust and stay joyful most of the time. However, after months of taking care of him with a lot of help and seeing our retirement savings disappear at the rate of several thousand dollars a month, my energy was exhausted. I was crying and feeling that I could not take any more. I prayed for a miracle. When God finally got through to me He said, "If you do not keep your joy flowing, you will not be able to handle this." That brought me up short, and since then I have been able to keep my joy flowing. I took care of him at home for two years, until his condition became so bad that I had to have twenty-four hours per day help. The help was undependable. He has had nursing home care since then, and I visit him several times a week.

For more than a year, I prayed for God to miraculously restore Stan's body and mind to its former condition, and I encouraged him to believe for a miracle. At the spring 1997 women's retreat, the main speaker told all of us to get alone that afternoon and "ask God what He is to you."

I followed instructions on a walk in the woods and asked, "Lord, I think I know what you are to me, but in obedience to the speaker I am asking what you are to me."

There was already a strong anointing on me as I walked and prayed, but as I stood by a beautiful stream and asked that question, the anointing increased. God said, "I am your Comforter. I have been your Comforter all of your life, (naming time after time) and I will be your Comforter when I take Stan from you."

I asked, "Then you are not going to give me a miracle?"

He said, "No. I am working on his sanctification, and that is what I want you to pray for. When I have finished that, I will take him to be with me."

Five more years have passed since He told me that, and I have not seen much evidence of spiritual growth, but I have to trust that it is taking place. Stan always likes to have me read the Bible to him and other books that encourage spiritual growth, and he welcomes my prayers. He enjoys the little weekly services our home group hosts bring to him, but there is so much mental confusion that I wonder how much he can take in. I feel so sorry for the constant pain he suffers and the dull life he lives in the nursing home that sometimes I pray that God will hasten the sanctification so he can go to heaven where I know he would be so much happier.

I have read several books to him of experiences people have had when they had death or near death experiences and have been brought back. Some have had brief glimpses of heaven, or a few, of hell. I have also read several books about experiences others have had in visions of heaven. The one we liked the best was Jesse Duplantis' book, *Heaven*, when God took him in a six-hour vision to heaven, probably like the one Paul wrote about. The explanation of the trinity in the book is very understandable. The assurance that we will have important work to do there, for which we are preparing now in this life, was a joyful confirmation to me of Jesus' parable of the talents.

Stan is interested in all of this and shows interest in wanting the spiritual growth promoted in the Bible and in these books. In spite of his confusion, he asks intelligent questions about what I read to him.

I can see in all of the terror that may be facing us after the September 11 disaster that we are all going to have to abide in God's love and care in order to know and do His will. We must pray that we will not only be safe, but that we may bring down that great anointing on our churches that we will need in order to bring in that final harvest.

On November 23, 2001, in prayer at home, I thought I heard God say that there will be another national crisis and that those who pretend to be our friends now will not turn out to be our friends in the end. I understood this to refer to nations that are now going along with our war on terrorists. This may have been my own thinking because of what we are living through.

That night at the Saturday meeting, I believe the Lord said, "When the national crisis comes, there will be standing room only in churches. Keep pressing in to me until my Spirit comes down like fire so that you can be one of those churches with standing room only."

I asked how long we would have to press in, because it seemed to me that we had been doing that for some time. He said, "Until the fire comes. I did not say that it would be easy. If this little group will persist in pressing in to me, the desire to pray will spread to the whole church."

I was still wondering how long, and He reminded me that when I was a child, we heard that the Indians started fires by rubbing two sticks together until they got sparks. We tried to do it but could not. I understood that He meant that we would have to work hard at this and persist until revival breaks out.

At our Saturday night prayer meeting, December 8, 2001, I was praying fervently for God to manifest His presence in our church in any way He chose. I named a few spectacular ways in which He had manifested His presence in churches where great revival has broken out. Lisa Otis said that while I was praying this way the Lord said to her, "The way I would prefer to manifest My presence would be for you to love one another."

Sons of God

I told them that this reminded me of a Benny Hinn program that week with Tommy Tenney. Tenney had felt led to wipe the dust from Benny's shoes as an act of servant attitude. They had agreed that the coming move of the Holy Spirit across America would come as a result of the body of Christ loving and serving one another.

On December 19, 2001, I was praying alone for revival while I waited for Jeanette to come for our prayer time together. A strong anointing came on me while I was speaking in tongues. I mentally heard the word "flood," and I asked, "God, what kind of flood are you telling me about?"

I could see water everywhere and knew people and things were being swept away or ruined. God said, "A flood of economic disaster with increasing depression, many people will have everything they own and are proud of swept away."

I said, "Lord, people are saying that the recession will soon be over. If things get worse, the liberal Democrats will win the coming elections and be back with their tax and spend and giveaway programs."

He said, "They can't. There will not be money for that. The money that is available will be used for the war. The war will get worse."

He reminded me of my prophetic dream of coming poverty and of George Washington's vision. While at Valley Forge in the winter of 1777, George Washington saw a vision of three wars with much fighting, death and destruction in our country. Each war was incited by a dark cloud and overcome by a white cloud. The first was the fight for Independence from England, that he was fighting in. The second was the Civil War, North and South fighting over an influence from Africa. The third will be an invasion from Europe, Asia and Africa. Many American cities and towns will be destroyed. George Washington saw rebuilding and survival of our nation after each war.

God said, "Do not be afraid, just trust me, and I will take care of you. This is important. You must stay close to me and have absolute confidence that I am with you and will guide you and take care of you no matter what is happening around you. If you will trust me, you will have joy and peace and be a blessing to many others who are afraid."

God said that the great revival we are praying for and expecting will come during this time of trial because people are desperate for answers to their troubles. Some will turn to Him, but others will turn away and be destroyed.

Jeanette arrived, and as I went to let her in I said, "God if you really said all of that, please let Jeanette get the same message."

I said to her, still with that powerful anointing on me, "I find it hard to believe what I think the Lord has been saying to me." I suddenly started speaking in tongues again, and when I finished, I said, "I believe God wants you to interpret."

After a brief pause, she gave an interpretation assuring us of God's love and his appreciation of what we are trying to do and that He will take care of us through all of the terrible things that are about to happen. We will not have all that we would like to have, but He will see that we have all that we need. He wants us to have no fear, but to be sure that we stay close to Him and give strength to hurting people around us.

I said that I did not understand why, if this is true, we are not hearing it from Christian leaders we hear on television. They just talk about the great revival they expect and say is already beginning. David Wilkerson has been almost the only one warning of coming economic and other disasters. Jeanette said that she would guess that a lot of little people like us are hearing God's warning on this.

The following afternoon I received David Wilkerson's periodical letter and copy of a sermon in the mail. In the letter, he quoted a message God gave him during a time of awesome silence in his Times Square Church:

> Very fearful times are just ahead. Even now, while the nation and the city are still in fear, there are great calamities still to come to America. I warn you because I love you, and I want you to draw near to me. When you hear these sudden things, you are not to fear. My Word says men's hearts shall fail them for fear. But when you see these sudden things coming upon the nation and upon this city, you are not to fear; you are to run to Me in your mind and in your heart. Immediately run to Me and My embrace, because I will keep you. I will hold you safe in My arms, if you will be in confidence and faith in Me and be not afraid. This will be your testimony in the days ahead; that around you on the job, on the subways, everywhere you go, people are literally going to break down and weep and cry, "Why, why, why?" Even

now they do so. But you are not to cry, "Why?" You are to say, "Even so, come Lord Jesus."

So be not afraid! More, much more, is to come, frightening the whole world. But My people will rise up in faith. And I promise that if you will trust Me, I will keep you from the wicked one. I will keep you from the spirit of this age; I will send angels to walk with you and guard you. And no weapon formed against you shall prosper.

In a letter shortly after this one, David Wilkerson said that the Lord had revealed to him that we will have a brief recovery from the present economic recession, and then there will be an economic collapse that will last a long time. On the twenty-seventh, when Jeanette came for our weekly prayer time, I showed her David Wilkerson's letter concerning the message he received during the Times Square Church service and we both laughed. She said in the midst of her laughter, "If it is going to be so terrible, why are we laughing?" In the midst of my laughter, I said, "Because we know we heard from God."

Later, while each of us was praying silently, I felt she had a vision and asked her whether she did. She said, "Not really. I was praying for a lot of different people, but all the time I was seeing myself with a coffee can reaching behind me into a large barrel of beans I had purchased to give away in the depression, and I wasn't worried about the supply giving out. It just kept growing, and I kept handing the beans out to people in need."

I asked whether she knew that this kind of thing had happened in modern times. She was surprised, so I told her about a group from a Roman Catholic Church in Central America that I heard about several years ago on Trinity Broadcasting Network who decided to help the people who lived on the city dump and got most of their food there. This Catholic group gave them a Christmas dinner. They prepared food for one hundred people, but more than twice that many came, so they just prayed for God to supply the need and kept handing out food. They had so much food left over that they were able to take it to orphanages and hospitals. This experience inspired them to continue helping the poor. Everyone in their group was expected to help with the work. Old ladies who could not work sat alongside and prayed for the supply. The food supply grew as they handed it out. An Episcopal priest's wife, who was sharing in the TV program, said she watched a pile of tomatoes grow as the workers picked up tomatoes.

Jeanette was delighted to think that she may be able to experience her vision when things get worse. This started me remembering other somewhat similar experiences that I was able to tell her about in our next meeting.

Some of us from the Northern Lights wanted to have our first Christmas dinner together. With our children, there were eighteen for dinner. We had finished the main meal and were ready for desert, three chocolate pies that Dorothy had made. Just then eleven more people dropped in on their way to their home in Oregon. Our hostess assumed that since it was already dark they would not stay long, so we sang Christmas Carols and visited and visited and visited.

Finally, Jane summoned two helpers to serve the pies. They tried to figure out how to divide three pies into twenty-nine pieces, but there was no way. So they prayed for God's help and just started cutting and serving slices of pie. Of course, the rest of us knew nothing of their dilemma. When someone set a slice of pie on the card table in front of me, I thought it was the strangest slice of chocolate pie I had ever seen. It was very narrow, but it was as high as a two-layered cake and there was something shimmery about it. It was as if I was seeing a vision. I ate it and found it was very filling. Later, I asked Dorothy what kind of pans she baked those pies in to make them so high. She said, "Dixie, they were just ordinary chocolate pies. God multiplied them, and we had two-thirds of a pie left after serving twenty-eight people. Only one person refused a slice."

I remembered a story that Dennis Bennett's wife, Alberta, told of a Sunday afternoon when several people dropped in for an unexpected visit right after she put a casserole in the oven that was just big enough for her small family. Dinnertime came and her husband invited their guests to eat with them, not knowing the problem he was creating for her. She had nothing in the house that she could add to that meal, so she prayed over her casserole and set it on the table. It fed twelve people with a little left over, and everyone had enough.

SONS OF GOD

There was another strange story. I heard about an experience of a prayer warrior who prayed for civilian prisoners of our enemies during World War II. She had heard that they were being kept in terrible conditions with very little food of poor quality. She prayed daily for God to supply good food for them. After the war, she happened to meet some of those former prisoners, and one of them said to her, "Oh, you are the woman who brought us food every evening."

At the end of this meeting with Jeanette, I handed her the December/January newsletter from End Time Handmaidens, Inc., which had just come. It had a prophecy by Sister Gwen Shaw that confirmed what we have been receiving from God on the hard times coming and the revival resulting from that. It was a long message, but the gist of it was that nothing would be the same throughout the world after the September 11 terrorist attack. America will be kept on its knees. We will go from sorrow to sorrow, trial to trial, and grave to grave, but in the midst of all this, our country will experience our greatest revival. She warned that no one will escape the attack of the enemy; and we must prepare to be instruments God can use to open his storehouse of help to the hurting—to be as Joseph in the Egyptian famine. We must be mightily filled with the Holy Ghost and prepare to subdue kingdoms and work works of righteousness, taking back souls from the enemy.

On February 28, I received in the 700 Club's Fact File a report of Pat Robertson's personal annual prayer retreat December 27-31, 2001, in which he always seeks (through prayer and fasting) for God's guidance for his personal life and ministry. He also asks for any insights that God chooses to give him for the nation and the world.

God showed him through Scripture that the task of His servants was to turn men and women from sin to righteousness. Then God said, "Argentina is in financial collapse. Worldwide recession or depression is possible as economic shock waves hit every country. One more September 11-style attack and the United States will go over the economic edge. America will never be the same again."

On December 30, Pat Robertson received this word:

> This year there will be a false sense of optimism about America's strength and the economy. People will forget the tragedy. It will be

life as usual, business as usual. Then the terrors will begin. There will be panic and the screams and crying of the dying. Whether they will listen or not, you must warn them to turn to me and turn from sin.

The revival that has started in the hearts of a few will continue to bear fruit and grow. I know how to make a difference between those who are mine and those who are not."

The Israelis will accommodate Arafat to their own sorrow. Sharon is indecisive. He has missed his opportunity. Now it is too late.

I will put my mantle over George Bush to protect him. He talks to me and I will lead him.

America will not survive what is coming in its present form. The proud will be humbled. Then they will turn to me and I will lift them up.

CBN is entering its greatest ministry. As people are gripped by terror, they will turn to a source of answers. Stay close to me and I will provide the word for the people.

Then Pat gave Scriptures the Lord gave him on his judgment of the wicked and help to the righteous in Isaiah 3:10 and Isaiah 5.

In August 2008, John Paul Jackson made public a vision he received which indicates we are currently in a ten year period which can be described as a "Perfect Storm." He believes that the horrible things which have been and will take place in the United States and the whole world are not God's judgment but God's mercy, so that many more people will turn to God.

I remembered that in Deuteronomy 17:6 God said that at the mouth of two or three witnesses a person worthy of death should be put to death. If this is so in a thing as serious as this, surely we should accept the witness of such great leaders as David Wilkerson, Gwen Shaw, Pat Robertson, and John Paul Jackson, especially since we repeatedly get the same messages that we feel are coming from God. If you, the reader, will ask God whether these are valid warnings, and you are open to believe whatever He chooses to say to you, I know He will answer you.

Chapter 17

Lord of the Storms

WE HAVE HAD increasing evidence that weather conditions all over the world could bring more and more destructive storms, tornadoes, and hurricanes. The Lord Himself tells us that natural disasters will be one of the things that will drive us to our knees. We should be learning now how to protect ourselves from these things by trusting Him to guide us and how to pray during disasters of all kinds. The apostles learned from experience that, "Even the winds and the sea obey him [Jesus]" (Matt. 8:27). Some of us have learned by our own experiences that God will give us some control over weather through our guided prayers. I will give a few examples of my experience in praying about weather, even in requests for small favors.

In June 1961, I invited the women in our Northern Lights to bring their children and join me and mine for a day-and-a-half of fun at our cabin on Lake Roessiger. We prayed for good weather, knowing that almost without fail there was at least a little rain every day for the first two weeks of June. As soon as school was out for the year, we arrived in the late afternoon expecting to have an outdoor picnic with hot dogs and toasted marshmallows. Dark clouds were banked up against the mountains, the sky was gray, and drops of rain were falling.

Jane said to me, "This is not right. Let's go down on the dock and pray."

Sons of God

We stood on the dock and petitioned the Lord for enough clear weather to have our picnic. It occurred to me that Jesus commanded the storm to stop, so I decided to do likewise. I pointed to the dark clouds against the mountains and made a small circular motion with my forefinger then pointed toward the south while speaking. "You rain clouds turn around and head south as fast as you can go and clear this sky so we can have sunshine for this picnic."

We stood with our mouths open in amazement as those clouds made a fast circular turn and then leaped one after another as fast as frightened sheep racing for cover. The sky cleared, and we had sunshine for the whole of our picnic. As soon as we went indoors, the rain came. We experienced the same thing for the next day and a half. At our request, it was clear when we were outdoors and raining when we were inside. The children shared in our delight at how God answered our prayers and gave us good fellowship.

On our last morning, there was a steady downpour while we had breakfast and packed to go home after lunch. The children were getting restless. At eleven o'clock I stood at the window looking at the hopeless downpour and asked, "Lord, could you please give us sunshine long enough for the children to have one last swim?" Immediately the sun came out. I turned to the children and said, "Get your swim suits on quickly. I have just asked the Lord to give us sunshine just long enough for you to have a last swim." Of course, they were delighted to obey that order. They had an hour of fun in the lake in full sun. When the last child stepped onto the porch, the clouds covered the sun and the rain poured again all through lunchtime.

On Friday evening, September 12, 1962, the Northern Lights met for our usual weekly prayer and praise time together. As usual, we were excited about what the Lord would do. We had some concern about the weather because a storm was moving up from Oregon with winds reported to be over one-hundred miles per hour. The last report was that its speed was lessening and would not be that strong by the time it reached Seattle. We learned later that it was still one-hundred miles per hour when it reached us.

The meeting was as lively as ever, with a lot of singing and reports on "what God did this week." Then we settled down for Bible study and prayer for special needs. About 8:30 rain pounded on the roof and against the windows in bursts of fury. Then the loud snapping of limbs breaking from trees next door interrupted our thoughts. I tried to quiet my fears, but could not.

"I can't stand this any longer," I said. "Let's pray for the safety of everyone and everything we care about."

"Yes, let's do."

"Shall we call home?"

"It might upset them more if they know we are worried. They know where we are if they want to be in touch. Let's just pray."

We knelt in a circle and held hands, praying in turn for all of our loved ones and our homes and other property, for our church and pastor, friends, and the city. We calmed each other with words of faith. Our feeling on parting after the storm subsided was that it was in God's hands, and He has been good to us, so why worry.

We rejoiced over telephone calls the next morning as we reported to each other that everyone important to the group was safe and the only sign of the storm around our homes was a few small limbs broken from trees. However, we learned that there had been extensive damage to buildings and homes all over the city and that power interruptions had occurred in some areas.

Stan and I decided to take our children to Lake Roessiger to see whether there was damage to the cabin. Steve invited his friend, Margaret Ann, to go with us. She was only seven, but she had spent so much time with us that I felt like she was my friend too.

On the thirty-five mile drive to the lake, we were repeatedly shocked at the sight of big trees on the road, on power lines, or over crushed buildings. Workmen were busy clearing a path for the cars. The last such scene was just a half-mile from our cabin. We turned off the main highway dreading what we might see at the end of our little access road.

Miracle of miracles, the cabin was still standing, and so were all of our trees. We scattered in all directions to investigate. The others went eastward as I walked west, inspecting each of five cabins.

I spoke aloud to the Lord, "It's so strange. All of that damage on the way up, and I cannot find even a leaf or a twig out of place here. Is it possible that the big hill protected us, or that the storm was turned aside just up the road, or did you really work a miracle for us and our special friends?"

I walked out on our dock and looked across the lake, searching for damage on the other side, but saw none. Margaret Ann joined me and sat down on the bench. She spread her arms in a circular motion indicating the land across the lake. "You see all the trees that are broken and bent?"

"No, Margaret Ann. I do not see any damage. I walked up that way and did not find one thing disturbed. I wonder if the storm just stopped back there where we saw the tree over the cabin roof."

"You are wrong," she said. "Steve and I went this way, and there are lots of big limbs down, and bushes torn up. There are lots of big trees down and one smashed a cabin right down to the ground. It's just two cabins that way."

She made a small circle with her finger, pointing to our cabin and those on either side. "It's like a quiet little country in the middle of a big noisy city."

I remembered my question to the Lord, and his silent presence told me that he had sent this little messenger to answer me. I knew that I would always cherish this fragile moment. I said, "If that's the way it is, Margaret Ann, we should be very grateful to God."

Her face relaxed in a satisfied expression. "Yes."

I cannot remember the name of a very destructive hurricane that swept through the south from Florida to Louisiana sometime in the 1980s, but I followed the news about it for anxious hours. I was up all night watching the news and praying. I was especially concerned when it was heading straight for Metarie and New Orleans and suburban cities because I had one half-sister in Metarie and another in New Orleans together with their families plus old friends in the path of that storm. It seemed to be sure to hit Metarie and New Orleans with a wind speed of 135 miles an hour. Finally, just before six o'clock, I heard the report that the velocity was decreasing and it was going to skirt around Metarie and New Orleans. At that point, I was able to go to bed and to sleep. I am sure that there were hundreds of people, possibly thousands, who were praying for safety for themselves or others.

Lord of the Storms

I have had numerous experiences of praying for guidance to have friends or relatives visit from out of state at a time when the weather would be good. They have almost always come during an especially good time. Even when they have come when it is drippy and overcast, God has granted my request for a clear sky at the most needed times so that they can see the beauty of our environment. Our name, the Evergreen State, is appropriate, but a lot of rain is required to keep our many evergreen trees healthy and our many lakes, rivers, and streams filled and flowing.

If our loving God is so willing to grant our requests for good weather and freedom from destruction in storms, we should have all the more confidence that He will preserve us through any natural disaster. He will also watch over all who truly trust in Him and are willing to follow His plan for our lives and ministry through war or terrorism.

Chapter 18

Distractions, Offenses, and Forgiveness

THE FOLLOWING NUMBERED points are a summary from George Otis Jr.'s sermon at our church on June 6, 2002. In his research with the Sentinel Group on churches and communities that have experienced revival and transformation by the power of God, the following were found to be true in each situation. Since we are praying for God to come in and make us like the churches in the book of Acts—with all of the signs that Jesus said would follow believers (see Mark 16:17-18)—we may be helped by pursuing the following conditions taken from the sermon:

1. Those praying for revival invited God to come into their church and community. This does not come with a mass of people praying. It does not take the whole church or whole community of churches.
2. We need united prayer, not unanimous prayer. We can have united prayer where two or three are gathered in God's name with clean hands and pure hearts. God is looking for small committed clusters.
3. Ask God to increase our spiritual appetites to make us thirsty for His presence. Ask Him to come feed us, to provoke a hunger and thirst for Him, to empty us of our satisfaction with things as they are, in us and in our community or nation. Ask Him

to make us desperate for revival and for the transformation of our society, to convict us of our need for social change, to make us see the sins in society so clearly that we are desperate for transformation.

4. Ask Him to reveal our own hearts, where we need to change, and our motives in asking Him to come. Are we asking Him to come so that He can do something for us, or because we want His presence and His will to be accomplished in our lives? He must transform us before He can transform the community.

5. To attract the Holy Spirit, we must familiarize ourselves with His character and His ways. God is attracted to the fruit of the Spirit and to righteous choices, not to the honey of giftedness and stature. He wants broken, contrite followers inwardly transformed, open to His will.

6. Ask God to devastate us, to devastate all of our strongholds, to bring us to the point of emptiness, dependence, and helplessness upon anything of our own.

7. Ask God to stimulate a hunger for Him in others in our church and community.

8. Ask Him to increase our spiritual stamina so that we pray fervently for revival and do not give up until the fire of revival is ignited.

9. We were created with a spiritual hunger for God, but we try to satisfy that hunger with the wrong kinds of food. Two things keep us from reaching our goal of revival. One is internal offenses, and the other is external distractions. We need some wholesome diversions, but we can push off a lot of what is available to us in order to spend time with God. We are easily offended by others. We hold on to the offenses, nurture and talk about them to others and share offenses with each other. We should instead forgive, love and pray for the offenders. Ask God to help us focus on and change in these two areas, external distractions and internal offenses.

I am sure that all nine points are important if we are to have clusters of prayer warriors with clean hands and pure hearts praying to bring a

Distractions, Offenses, and Forgiveness

transforming revival that will bring in a great harvest of souls. I would guess that the ninth has been a lifelong struggle for most of us.

George Otis said in his sermon:

> We struggle to fight off the magnetic pull of the world. When I use the word "world," I am not just talking about all of the nasty things. I am talking about all of the shiny glittery things. Everywhere we look there are things that are not sinful but compete for our time and attention and draw time that could be invested in getting desperate before God, activities that are not sinful but do not move us forward either. I am not saying that there is not a place for wholesome diversions. You will burn out. God has designed us so that we need a Sabbath, but there is a very high percentage of legitimate distractions of our society that we can push off. The world is pulling us into the sand pit. We have got to move back and get a hold of God and not let Him go.
>
> The other problem we face is our internal offenses. We are very easily offended by our friends, spouses, parents, children, people in the church, our pastors, coworkers, political leaders, by just about everybody. We have full offense industries. We would not have talk shows on radio and TV if it were not for all of the grudges and offenses that people nurture and hold. One of my favorite speakers and teachers, British Campbell MacAlpine, said, "Offended people attract offended people."
>
> I have noticed it in this church. They talk about their grievances and how they have been wronged. It is going on in most churches today. This is how church divisions start. Somebody allows an offense to take root in his or her heart. Offended people attract each other, and before you know it you have a church split. One thing I would like to do. There is a little booklet and an audio tape I would like to distribute titled, "No offense" by Campbell MacAlpine about not allowing offense to take root in our lives. I know how easy it is. It can be a look or somebody did not choose you for a position you felt you were qualified for. The very fact that you took offense proves you were not qualified. So let's ask God to help us focus on these two areas, external distractions and internal offenses. Let's ask God to help us learn to shed offenses, to not take them upon ourselves.

I, Dixie, want to share what I hope God is trying to teach me about external distractions and internal offenses. He is still trying to teach me to spend at least an hour a day in God-inspired prayer. I am able to do this most days and sometimes pray for two or three hours, but rarely more. The longer prayer time is great in the anointing. He has admonished me to spend less time reading and watching TV, even though I am careful about the content.

Some days are so busy with things I need to do that it is hard to make prayer time, so I sympathize with people who have young families and have jobs. However, I know from experience that it is worth making the time. When I was facing the gross problems that can come with raising teenagers, I would pray lengthy desperate prayers for them and for God's guidance, sometimes with the help of a friend during a crisis. Then when things smoothed out, I would think that now I could relax and spend less time in prayer, but another crisis was sure to come. Finally, I realized that I had better stay prayed up so that I could handle the crisis when it came.

Around that time, I read a book by Star Daley in which he said that if you want God's guidance all of the time, you must come into His presence at the beginning of each day. He recommended that you spend time in prayer before you do anything else and pray until you feel a strong sense of His presence, whether it takes fifteen minutes or an hour or two. At that point you are ready to handle the problems of the day if you stay in His will and continue to feel that presence and obey God's guidance.

I cannot say that I immediately handled that challenge, but in these latter years of my life, I seem to feel that presence just about all of the time. I wake up and automatically begin speaking in tongues and speaking to the Lord. Those wake-up prayers are probably all praise, and Scripture tells us that God dwells in the praise of His people. We feel His presence most when we praise and trust Him to take care of everything.

Psalm 91:1 tells us, "He that dwelleth in the secret place of the most High shall abide under the shadow of the Almighty." That dwelling and abiding in His presence gives us the confidence that He will keep all of the promises that follow in that psalm. There are many stories of individuals and companies of troops who have come safely through battles of all kinds when they daily claimed all of the promises of that psalm.

Distractions, Offenses, and Forgiveness

Offenses are probably the hardest things most of us have to learn to handle. We were born thinking that the world revolves around us. The baby and young child demand our attention. The new Christian thinks of a spiritual principle he is learning in terms of how it relates to or benefits himself. However, God is trying to teach us to die to self, to let go of our own wills and our own support of self-interests and let Him teach us how to serve the interests of others.

God wants to save as many people as He can, not just us. He wants us to learn to live the cross principle in our personal lives and in our ministries. Jesus died to save the whole world, and His last command was to go into all the world and tell everyone what He did for them on the cross. Jesus urged His disciples to forget about their personal interests and serve and love each other, because if the world could see that spirit of self-sacrifice and love of others demonstrated in them, the world would want their God.

Because of several deaths in my family and other tragedies during my early childhood, I had a hard time handling emotions and reacted to offenses with deep hurt. As a young adult, I decided that I had to handle this kind of reaction. I would ask myself, "Now if I said or did what she did to me or about me, what would my motive be?" Of course, I would not have a bad motive, I thought, so I would attribute my supposed good motive to my offender and could thus excuse the offense.

During my education in psychology and social work and experience in working with difficult people as a social worker, I learned that, without a doubt, every person who is hard to live with or deal with has had a childhood that nobody would choose to live through. This helped me in dealing with difficult people in my personal life. However, this knowledge is not enough to solve personal problems. We have to follow Bible principles to find the real solution.

The one who offends you is, in your mind, your enemy. Jesus said, "Love your enemies, bless them that curse you, do good to them that hate you, and pray for them which despitefully use you, and persecute you; that you may be the children of your Father which is in heaven: for he maketh his sun to rise on the evil and on the good, and sendeth rain on the just and on the unjust" (Matt. 5:44-45).

SONS OF GOD

I believe that the one who taught me the most about the difficulty of following these instructions was my hot-tempered mother-in-law. Stan and I were having dinner together the evening we applied for our marriage license. He mentioned that his mother had, that afternoon, tried to talk him out of marrying me. Yet later during that meal, he said that he would like to have his mother live with us—that she was just a sweet little old lady who wanted nothing more than a chair in which to sit and read her newspaper.

I said that two women cannot run the same house, but I understood his desire to see his mother was properly cared for. I would, therefore, agree to having a house with an apartment for her, and I would help him meet his goal. Actually, in the years following, it was I who could identify with her needs and see that they were met. Her temper, however, was an ongoing problem.

A few weeks after we were married, during one of her visits to our apartment, she finally had to express verbally her angry objections to her observation of the fact that Stan and I were sharing the housekeeping chores. I was forcing her precious sonny boy to do women's work. He was finishing his college degree on the GI Bill, available to World War II veterans, and I was a caseworker at Washington Children's Home. We felt that our arrangement was fair to both of us. I walked out of the room and left Stan to deal with his mother. I could hear him lecturing her. He told me later that it was obvious that this was his mother's problem, not mine.

From this experience until her death at age 87, she never criticized me in Stan's presence. But she had many explosions when alone with me, her eyes blazing, spitting out venomous words of intense hatred. Yet at other times, she expressed her appreciation by telling me that I was the best friend she ever had or that I had done more for her than anyone she had ever known. Stan never knew about this problem because she was always sweet and gracious when the rest of the family was present, and most of the time with me alone.

I could understand her problem because she had a very hard childhood and two failed marriages. She was alone and obviously had hoped that Stan would devote himself to her and never marry. However, this did not help me face the tirades. I handled them with a smiling gracious exterior and a burning hatred inside. The veins in my neck were tense,

Distractions, Offenses, and Forgiveness

and I thought about it so much that I realized I had to do something about it before I developed a physical problem.

About the time I realized that I had to change my reactions in self-defense, a friend who did not know my problem told me how she solved her problem with her difficult mother-in-law who made frequent two-week visits to their home. She always arrived ready to straighten out the household her way. My friend endured it as I had, smiling on the outside and burning on the inside.

She finally told the Lord, "God, I hate that woman, but I choose to love her. I give you my will." She said that she prayed that prayer over and over, "I give you my will." Gradually, the Holy Spirit took over and she could actually love that difficult woman.

She said, "And you know, I found that she is not really that bad."

So I took the advice she had unknowingly given me and found that I could love poor little fearful hurting Edna. She had gone regularly to church much of her life and even learned to tithe. She told me three times that she was too wicked for God ever to forgive her. Each time I helped her say the sinner's prayer and assured her that she was forgiven. Even this did not put an end to the tirades.

I found that when she was angry, I could not reason with her. I would say, "I cannot deal with this now." I would walk away and let her work it out alone. After about three days, she would come down from her apartment and pat me on the cheek and say, "I'm so sorry."

I asked the Lord to let me be with her when she died so that I could help her through the experience. She was in a good nursing home when she died, and Stan, Colleen, and I were with her. The nurse indicated that it was almost over. Stan and Colleen were on one side of her bed, and the nurse and I on the other. I said, "Mom, Jesus is here to take you to be with Him. Take Jesus by the hand and go with Him." She took two more breaths and was quiet.

God's presence flooded the room, and Colleen, Stan, the nurse, and I hugged each other and cried. Later I asked the nurse if she felt the Presence. She said, "Oh, yes. It is always that way when a Christian dies, but it is terrible when an unbeliever dies. You would not want to be there."

Sons of God

We did not want to leave that Presence. We sat for a long time talking about the good things about Edna. Because of that experience, I know she is in heaven, and I am very glad I learned to love her.

One way I test whether I have really forgiven someone is to picture meeting that person in heaven. Will I be glad to see them and know I can fellowship with them for all of eternity? Or do I really hope I see them first so I can get busy elsewhere? First John 4:7-8 tells us, "Beloved, let us love one another: for love is of God; and every one that loveth is born of God, and knoweth God. He that loveth not knoweth not God; for God is love." In Jesus' teaching on loving our enemies in Matthew 5:48 he ended by saying "Be ye therefore perfect, even as your Father which is in heaven is perfect.

We can strive for perfection, and I believe this is what Paul meant in Philippians 2:12, "Work out your own salvation with fear and trembling." We are saved by faith, but we have to strive to change our souls (minds, wills, and emotions). I doubt that any of us will ever achieve perfection here, but our reward in heaven depends on the progress we make here. First Corinthians 3 tells us about the judgment of our works with rewards and the burning out of the things not acceptable in heaven. Our works will be revealed by fire, and only the good ones will survive and receive a reward.

First John 3:2 tells us, "Beloved, now are we the sons of God, and it doth not yet appear what we shall be: but we know that, when he shall appear, we shall be like him; for we shall see him as he is." Can it be that the fire that burns up our imperfections will be that knowledge of how perfect He is and how ashamed we are of our imperfections?

Paul tells us in Philippians 3:12-14 that he does not consider himself perfect but that he wants to forget those things that are behind [his past failures?], and press forward for the prize of the high calling of God in Christ Jesus. That high calling is perfection in love for God and others and a determination to serve others, not self. There is no other atmosphere in heaven, and anything else has to be burned out of us either here or at the judgment of saints.

It seems to me that most gossip is like the attitude of the Pharisee's prayer, thanking God that he is not like that publican or other men (see Luke 18:10-14). We can see other people's imperfections, and when we

DISTRACTIONS, OFFENSES, AND FORGIVENESS

tell others about them, we are implying that we are better than that. We may even use prayer for that person as an excuse to gossip. We should be very careful about reporting what we know because it will ruin somebody's reputation. What we say is repeated with ever-changing and worsening details.

We need to take any bad report and pray for guidance on what to do about it and be sure that our actions are God's will and that they are in keeping with Scripture. We need to really know the Bible to line our actions up with it.

Chapter 19

Strongholds to Be Broken

DURING CHERYL'S JANUARY 2002 teaching, we witnessed a few miracles of healing and deliverance, and her teaching was excellent. On the last night of teaching, she and George Otis ministered together. I asked him whether anyone was working on bringing down the strongholds of Satan in our area so that we can experience the transformation of this Puget Sound area such as has happened in a few places in the world where even the government has turned to God.

He said that plans are being made and studies undertaken of where the strongholds are and we will be told more about this later. The work of bringing down the strongholds will occur in about three years. In view of the dire predictions of coming disaster, I keep wondering whether three years will be soon enough. Is it possible that a widespread concerted prayer effort could bring down those strongholds? If so, who would organize it?

I have learned that in order to find out where demonic forces receive their authority to control a city, nation, group, or individual, we must know who was in control and able to give his, her, or their authority to the demonic forces. For years it has been thought that the first people to arrive in our area many centuries ago came in from the orient into what are now Alaska and Canada, and moved downward and outward to populate all of the Americas. Recently, some researchers believe there is evidence that the Native Americans moved into this area from the south. Whichever is true, they brought with them their worship of ancestors and demon spirits that they called gods, and they practiced slavery and the sacrifice of their own people in the worship of their gods. This gave the demonic forces the authority to control North, Central, and South America. It is and will be very hard to win people to Christ in any of these areas until we join with Christian Native Americans to bring down the strongholds that their ancestors granted to demons.

These strongholds are joined by those of the later settlers from Europe, who came to the Northwest with a motive of greed and took unfair advantage of Native Americans. They also brought prostitution, gambling, and many other evil practices. Their descendants need to repent and be reconciled to Native Americans and join together to cast down all of their combined strongholds on the area.

A similar effort is being made in the New England area of our country to bring down the strongholds. Someone had a message from God that this is the womb of our country, because this is where the first European settlers entered, and they were the ones who started our United States.

I was praying one day about our country, and off to the side I had a vision of a very large womb and a very large syringe pumping something into the womb. I asked what God was trying to show me. He said that the womb of America must be cleansed. He then showed me a vision of the eastern part of our country with a wide strip along the coast in a bright highlight from Maine through Virginia. He said, "This is the womb of America, not just New England."

He said that some of the Europeans brought in Christianity, but others brought Masonic influences, and the Statue of Liberty is the Babylonian goddess. The settlers intermarried with the Native Americans and mixed cultures with them. Slaves were brought in from Africa, and in order to unite the thirteen colonies into one nation, this was accepted in our Constitution. The slaves brought in their demon gods, and there was another mixing in procreation and culture. Therefore, the descendants of all these cultures need to repent and join together in casting down the strongholds in order to have a transforming experience to bring our country under God's authority. It was the Civil War that set the slaves free, but we still have the scars from the war and the slavery. These strongholds must be dealt with through joint forgiving prayer also.

If this book is printed, I hope every reader will learn to spend at least an hour a day in concentrated prayer and develop the ability to recognize God's voice and live in His presence. If the predicted natural and manmade disasters really happen, every believer will need to learn now how to hear from God so that God's voice in our minds will be clear in His attempts to guide us out of danger's way. Even if all of the predictions of coming disasters do not come to pass, we need individual guidance to carry out our part of God's plan to bring in the great harvest of souls that are ready now for this final harvest. In addition, I hope that you will all join with those of us who are praying for our nation, that we may truly become what God intended us to be as a light of His love and saving power toward all the world.

WinePressPublishing
Your Book, Defined.
Since 1991.

To order additional copies of this book call:
1-877-421-READ (7323)
or please visit our website at
www.WinePressbooks.com

If you enjoyed this quality custom-published book,
drop by our website for more books and information.

www.winepresspublishing.com
"Your partner in custom publishing."